AF448969

BALZAC

LECTOR HOUSE PUBLIC DOMAIN WORKS

This book is a result of an effort made by Lector House towards making a contribution to the preservation and repair of original classic literature. The original text is in the public domain in the United States of America, and possibly other countries depending upon their specific copyright laws.

In an attempt to preserve, improve and recreate the original content, certain conventional norms with regard to typographical mistakes, hyphenations, punctuations and/or other related subject matters, have been corrected upon our consideration. However, few such imperfections might not have been rectified as they were inherited and preserved from the original content to maintain the authenticity and construct, relevant to the work. The work might contain a few prior copyright references as well as page references which have been retained, wherever considered relevant to the part of the construct. We believe that this work holds historical, cultural and/or intellectual importance in the literary works community, therefore despite the oddities, we accounted the work for print as a part of our continuing effort towards preservation of literary work and our contribution towards the development of the society as a whole, driven by our beliefs.

We are grateful to our readers for putting their faith in us and accepting our imperfections with regard to preservation of the historical content. We shall strive hard to meet up to the expectations to improve further to provide an enriching reading experience.

Though, we conduct extensive research in ascertaining the status of copyright before redeveloping a version of the content, in rare cases, a classic work might be incorrectly marked as not-in-copyright. In such cases, if you are the copyright holder, then kindly contact us or write to us, and we shall get back to you with an immediate course of action.

HAPPY READING!

BALZAC

EDGAR EVERTSON SALTUS

ISBN: 978-93-90198-92-4

Published: 1884

© 2020
LECTOR HOUSE LLP

LECTOR HOUSE LLP
E-MAIL: lectorpublishing@gmail.com

BALZAC

BY

EDGAR EVERTSON SALTUS

1884

CONTENTS

BALZAC.

CHAPTER I.

THE VAGARIES OF GENIUS.

"Great minds are bravely eccentric; they scorn the beaten track." —GOLDSMITH.

In the city of Tours, in whose gabled streets there lingers still some memory of la belle Impéria, Honoré de Balzac was born on the 20th of May, 1799.

His childhood was in no wise extraordinary, save for the avidity with which he read the Bible and the keen delight which he took in the possession of a little red violin. He was indifferent to romps and games, and when not lost in the mysterious depths of the Scriptures he played by the hour on his fiddle, and extracted therefrom an enjoyment which was almost sensual in its intensity. His parents were well-considered people, in easy circumstances. Honoré was their first-born, and to him were subsequently given two sisters and a brother, concerning whom only a passing mention need be made. His eldest sister, Laure, became the wife of M. de Surville, a civil engineer, survived her illustrious brother, and published his letters, together with a weak sketch of his life; his second sister also married, but died at an early age; while his brother Henri sought his fortune, after the manner of younger sons, in the colonies, failed to find it, and was otherwise entirely uninteresting.

At the age of eight, Balzac was placed as boarder at the Collége de Vendôme, where, through the compression of his dreamy nature by unaccustomed tasks and rules, he soon lapsed into a careless neglect of his duties, and became, in consequence, one of the most frequently punished pupils in his class. Favored, however, by the tacit connivance of a tutor, he passed most of his time in the library. Science, philosophy, belles-lettres, religion, history, and even dictionaries, he read and inwardly digested, and during the six years that he remained at the school he assimilated the substance of all the books worth reading.

This absorption of ideas produced a noteworthy effect. His eye embraced six or eight lines at a time, and his mind appropriated the thought with a velocity equal to his glance; a single word in a phrase often sufficing for a clear understanding of the whole.

His memory was like a vise. He remembered not only the ideas which he had acquired in reading, but also those which conversation and reflection had suggested. Words, names, figures, and places he not only recalled at will, but he saw them within himself, brilliant and colored as they were at the moment when he had first perceived them.

Mentally fortified by his extensive reading, he wrote at the age of twelve the famous "Traité de la Volonté," so often mentioned in his later works, but which was confiscated by the regent as the probable cause of his neglect of the regular curriculum, and which Balzac says he doubtless sold for waste paper without recognizing the value of the scientific treasures whose germs were thus wasted in ignorant hands.

After this loss, more than terrible to a young imagination, Balzac sought consolation in verse, and wrote a poem on the Incas, commencing: "O Inca! roi infortuné et malheureux!" which, with the exception of his subsequent "Cromwell," was his sole familiarity with the peplum of the Muse; for, of the four sonnets in the "Illusions Perdues," the first and second are by Lassaily, the third is by Madame de Girardin, and the fourth by Gautier, while the poem in "Modeste Mignon" was the work of Gérard de Nerval.

From these secret and laborious studies, as well as from possible fermentation of ideas, Balzac fell into a sort of coma and nervous fever, which was singularly inexplicable to his masters and teachers. His parents were hastily summoned, and the precocious boy, now almost epileptic, was taken home, where rest and quiet gradually calmed the tumult in his brain, and restored the health and vivacity of boyhood. Little by little the results of his extraordinary labors became classified within his troubled mind, and to them were added other ideas of a less abstract nature; and in wandering on the banks of the Loire, or in attending the impressive ceremonies at the Cathedral of Saint-Gatien, he acquired not only a love of the beautiful, but also the sincere and abiding faith in religion with which he subsequently enriched the pages of the "Comédie Humaine." At home, as at school, however, his intelligence was entirely unsuspected, and his sister, Madame de Surville, relates that whenever he chanced to make a brilliant remark his mother would invariably say, "It is impossible, Honoré, for you to understand what you are talking about;" whereupon Honoré would laugh, without deigning to enter into any explanations.[1] His father, however, who was an inoffensive disciple of both Montaigne and Swift, had his own reasons for thinking well of his son, and decided that a child of his could never by any chance be a fool; and while at that time he saw nothing in the boy which promised any immediate celebrity, he nevertheless cherished a few vague hopes.

But the prescience which the father lacked had already visited the son. From time to time he stated that he would some day be famous, and this boast appeared so outrageously insulting to his brother and sisters that they punished him with every torture which childish ingenuity could invent.

Balzac's family soon after moved to Paris, where he again was placed at school. There, as at Vendôme, he gave no sign of future genius, and as before was regard-

---

[1] *Balzac*, by Madame de Surville. Calmann Lévy, Paris.

ed as an idler and a dullard.

His classes completed, he attended the lectures of Guizot, Cousin, and Ville-main, and his degree of bachelier-ès-lettres obtained, he entered a law office which Scribe had just quitted. Here he acquired that luminous insight to law and procedure which served him to such advantage in the varied litigations of his future world, and enabled him, years after, to plead, as Voltaire did for Calas, in defense of Sébastien Peytel, a former acquaintance, accused of the murder of his wife and servant. The case was lost, and his client convicted; but his oration was none the less superb, and his argument is still cited as one of the most brilliant efforts in the annals of the French bar.

His legal apprenticeship completed, it was naturally expected that he would follow the law as a profession, but Balzac had other ideas; he felt as did Corneille *e tutti quanti*, that his vocation was not such as is found in courts, and expressed a preference for a purely literary life.

"But," objected his father, "do you not know that in literature, to avoid being a slave, you must be a king?"

"Very well," Balzac replied, "king I will be."

After many arguments it was finally agreed that he should be allowed two years of probation; and as his family were about to return to the country, he was lodged in the Rue Lesdiguières, near the Bibliothèque de l'Arsenal, on an allowance of a hundred francs a month. His life there he has in "Facino Cane" described as follows:—

"I passed my days at the neighboring library. I lived frugally, for I had accepted all the conditions of that monastic life which is so necessary to students and thinkers. I seldom went out, and when I did a simple promenade was converted into a source of study, for I observed the customs of the faubourg, its inhabitants and their characters. As badly dressed as the workmen and as careless of decorum, I attracted no attention from them, and was enabled to mix among them and watch their bargains and disputes.

"Observation had become to me intuitive. It penetrated the spirit without neglecting the body, or rather it seized exterior details so clearly that it immediately went beyond them. It gave me the power of living the life of any individual upon whom it was exercised, and permitted me to substitute my personality for his, as did the dervish in the 'Thousand and One Nights' who had the power of occupying the body and soul of those over whom he pronounced certain words. When, therefore, between eleven and twelve at night, I encountered a workman and his wife returning from the theatre, I amused myself in following them from the Boulevard du Pont-aux-Choux to the Boulevard Beaumarchais. At first they would speak of the play which they had just witnessed. From that they would begin to talk of their own affairs, the mother dragging her child after her, listening neither to its complaints nor to its demands. The money which was to be paid to them was added, and then spent in twenty different ways. Then came the household details, murmurings on the excessive price of potatoes, the length of the winter, energetic discussions on the baker's bill, and finally little quarrels, in which they displayed their characters in picturesque words. While listening to them I espoused their life. I felt their rags on my back; my feet marched in their tattered shoes; their desires, their needs, all passed into my spirit, and mine into theirs: it was the dream of a waking man. With them I grew angry at their tyrannical masters or at their customers who made them come again and again without paying what they owed.

"To relinquish my identity, to become another through the intoxication of the moral faculties, and to play this game at will, such was my sole distraction. I have sometimes wondered if this gift was one of those faculties whose abuse leads to madness, but its causes I have never sought. I know, merely, that I possess and make use of it."

This ability to penetrate mentally the individuality of another is the evident explanation of the minuteness with which all of Balzac's characters are drawn, as well as the secret of their logical attitudes; for as in every-day life, while it is a question whether man is his own providence or is interwoven in a web of pre-ordained circumstances, yet in either case certain results are inevitable and a matter of statistic, so in Balzac there is no dodging of fate or shirking of consequences, and he is careful, in sending his own blood tingling through the veins of his creations, to surround them with the same laws to which he is himself subjected.

During his novitiate Balzac prepared a five-act tragedy in blank verse, entitled "Cromwell," a subject which it is curious to note was simultaneously chosen by Victor Hugo. At its completion, a professor of the École Polytechnique was requested to decide whether the lines contained a sufficient promise of genius to warrant a further pursuit of literary honors on the part of the young aspirant. The play, conscientiously examined, was deemed simply detestable, and the referee adjudged that Balzac might do what he would, but that literature was certainly not his vocation.

From this decision there was no present appeal; and while his mother and sisters begged him to engage in some other occupation, his father assured him that he would suppress his allowance should he persist in his intentions. Another perhaps would have yielded, but his pride and belief in his destiny made his resolution unalterable, and Balzac was left in solitary sadness to meditate on the coquetries of the Muse.

"I delighted," he says in "La Peau de Chagrin," "in the thought that I should live in the midst of tumultuous Paris in an inaccessible sphere of work and silence, in a world of my own, of books and ideas, where like the chrysalis I should build a tomb only to emerge again brilliant and famous.

"I took the chances of dying to live. In reducing existence to its actual needs, I found that three sous for *charcuterie* prevented me from dying of hunger and preserved my mind in a state of singular lucidity, while enabling me at the same time to observe the wonderful effects which diet produces on the imagination. My lodging cost three sous a day, I burned at night three sous' worth of oil, and for two sous more I heated my room with charcoal: and in this manner I lived in my aerial sepulchre, working night and day with such pleasure that study seemed the most beautiful theme, the happiest solution, of existence. The calm and silence necessary to the student possess an indescribable something which is as sweet and intoxicating as love, and study itself seems to lend a sort of magic to all that surrounds us. The forlorn desk on which I wrote, my piano, my bed, my chair, the zigzags of the wall-paper, — all these things became as though animated and humble friends, the silent accomplices of my future. Many a time I have communicated my soul to them in a glance, and often in looking at the broken moulding I encountered new developments of thought, some striking proof of my system, or words which I considered peculiarly fitted to express ideas almost untranslatable."

Balzac had not as yet any settled plan of work, but he tried his hand, while forming his style, at a quantity of comic operas, dramas, comedies, and romances, none of which, however, were accepted save by the gutter's sneering fatalist, the ragpicker.

After many fruitless attempts and knocks at many a door, Balzac succeeded at last in finding a publisher, but of a type seen only in opéra bouffe, who proffered in payment of a romance a promissory note with a year to run. Balzac of course had no choice. He wished to appear in print. The bargain was concluded, and the "Héritière de Birague" was produced. Then, under various pseudonyms, such as Lord R'hoone, the anagram of Honoré, Dom Rago, M. de Viellerglé, and Horace de Saint-Aubin, he produced a quantity of novels somewhat after the style of Pegault Lebrun, and yet so diverse in treatment that one of them, "Wann-Chlore,"[2] was attributed to a luminary of the Romantic school, and another, "Annette et le Criminel," was suppressed by the censorship. Some of these books, whose paternity he always denied, have since been collected under the title of "Œuvres de Jeunesse," but of the greater part no trace remains.

Exhausted by privations and worn with continued study, Balzac was obliged to return to his family, then established at Villeparisis, where, broken in mind and health, he sank into an almost hopeless dejection.

"Is this what you term life," he wrote[3] to his sister, — "this involuntary rotation and perpetual return of the same things? I am in the springtide of a flowerless life, and I long to have some charm thrown over my chill existence; for of what use is fortune and pleasure when youth is gone? Of what use is the actor's gown if he play no longer his part? Old age is a man who has dined and looks at others eat; and I, I am young, and I hunger before an empty plate—Laura, Laura, shall I, then, never realize my two immense desires, to be celebrated and to be loved?"

But Balzac soon wearied of this plaintive inactivity, and, fertile in projects, conceived the plan of printing Molière complete in one volume, and of following it with similar editions of the French classics. When these had appeared, he proposed, like Richardson, to produce his own works, and his illuminous imagination immediately foresaw new Clarissas issuing from the press.

The necessary working capital he procured from his family, who, though far from rich, were none the less glad to aid him in an enterprise for which literature would be abandoned and a legitimate business adopted.

[2] The present title is *Jane la Pâle*.
[3] *Correspondance de H. de Balzac*. Calmann Lévy, Paris, 1877.

But after the publication of Molière and La Fontaine, in each of which he inserted an elaborate and original introduction, he was obliged, through the cabals of the other publishers, to relinquish his plan, while burdened at the same time with a load of debt which oppressed almost every hour of his after life.

He was now absolutely without resources. The expense of a few sous attending the carriage of a letter, an omnibus ride, anything, in fact, which demanded the outlay of ready money, he was obliged to forego, and even remained in his garret that he might preserve as long as possible the only shoes which he owned.

"My sole possessions," he wrote to his sister, "are my books, which I cannot part with, and my good taste, which unfortunately for the rich cannot be bought. If I were in prison I should be happier; life then would cost me nothing, and in any event I could not be more of a captive than I am."

But the pecuniary loss which he had sustained, and which amounted to about 120,000 francs, served but as a stimulus to renewed activity; and resolving that he would recover from the printing press all that it had robbed him of, he commenced to seek some undiscovered vein of literary treasure, and in 1829 brought out "Le Dernier Chouan," the first romance which he considered worthy to bear his own name. Its ferocity and passion attracted great attention, and the public became at once favorably disposed toward him; but when, a few months later, the "Physiologie du Mariage" appeared, its success was not only instantaneous, but Balzac was heralded as a new Molière. He now emerged from quasi obscurity into the white light of fame. Publishers were submissive, praise was unstinted. He had realized the first of his immense desires, and had it not been for his weight of debt he might perhaps have been able to realize the other, but his time was not his own. He labored, if possible, more incessantly than ever, conceived the plan of the "Comédie Humaine," and from that time up to almost the day of his death produced a series of masterpieces which in point of interest and erudition form the most gigantic monument in the history of modern literature.

His work accompanied him wherever he went. He dreamed of it; he wrote while he ate; he traveled over the better part of Europe, and wrote while he traveled; he composed in the omnibus and in the street; and had he had a mistress he would, in all probability, have followed the example of Baudelaire, and composed in her arms. Thoroughly conscientious, he invariably visited the place where the scenes of a drama were to be located. "I am going to Alençon," he would say; "you know Mlle. Cormon[4] lives there;" or, "I am off for Grenoble; there is where M. Benassis[5] lives:" for it should be remembered that not only were Balzac's characters as realistically vivid to him as are the hallucinations of a neurosthene, but he invariably spoke of them as another would of friends and acquaintances. "Let us talk of realities," he one day said to Jules Sandeau, who had been speaking to him of an invalid relative, "let us talk about 'Eugénie Grandet;'" and at another time, when his sister asked for some information about Captain Jordy,[6] Balzac replied very simply, "I never knew the man before he came to Nemours, but if he interests

[4] *Les Rivalités..*
[5] *Le Médecin de Campagne.*
[6] *Ursule Mirouët.*

you, I will try to learn something of him." It was a long time before he was able to find a suitable husband for Mlle. Camille Grandlieu, and rejected all who were suggested to him. "They are not in the same set," he would say. "Chance alone can supply her with a husband, and chance is a commodity which a novelist should use but sparingly. Reality alone justifies the improbable, and the probable alone is permitted to us." But Mlle. de Grandlieu was not destined to braid St. Catherine's tresses, and afterwards, to Balzac's great delight, found a suitable husband in the person of the young Comte de Restaud,[7] who in spite of his mother's derelictions[8] was otherwise a very acceptable suitor.

After the place of his novel had been visited, viewed from every aspect, the customs noted and the localisms acquired, Balzac would return to Paris, shut himself up in a garret, — the garret has its poetry, — and for weeks and sometimes months at a time he would not only disappear entirely from view, but all trace of him would be lost.

At other times, he would lodge under an assumed name, which he imparted only to his most intimate friends. "My address," he wrote to Madame Carraud in 1834, "is always Madame Veuve Durand, 13, Rue des Batailles;" and in 1837, he wrote to Dablin, "To see the Widow Durand, a name must be given. Yours is on the list."

"The house," Gautier wrote,[9] "of the Widow Durand was as well guarded as the Garden of the Hesperides. Two or three passwords were exacted, and that they might not become vulgarized they were frequently changed. Among others, I recall the following. On telling the janitor that the season for prunes had arrived, the visitor was permitted to cross the threshold; to the servant who prowled about the head of the stairway, it was necessary to murmur 'I bring laces from Belgium;' and on assuring the valet de chambre that Madame Bertrand was in excellent health, the visitor was ushered into the great man's presence."

It was in the Rue des Batailles that the famous boudoir of the "Fille aux Yeux d'Or" actually existed; and though its luxury would not appear unusual to-day, it was, nevertheless, a source of continual wonder to his Bohemian friends, and his own description of it is not devoid of interest:[10] —

"One side of the boudoir formed a graceful semicircle, while in the centre of the other, which was perfectly square, there shone a mantel-piece of marble and gold. The door, which was concealed behind a rich portière of tapestry, was directly in front of the window.

"In the horseshoe was a Turkish divan, fifty feet in circumference and as high as a bed. The covering was of white cashmere tufted with bows of black and lilac silk, which were disposed as at the angles of a lozenge.

"The back of this immense bed rose several inches above a pile of cushions,

---

[7] *Gobseck.*

[8] *Le Père Goriot.*

[9] *Honoré de Balzac,* par Théophile Gautier. Un volume in-18, chez Poulet-Malanis, 1859.

[10] *La Fille aux Yeux d'Or.*

which added to the general effect by their coloring and artistic arrangement.

"The boudoir was hung with a red material, over which was draped an Indian muslin fluted like a Corinthian column by a piping alternately hollow and round, and bordered at top and bottom by a band of lilac embroidered with black arabesques. Beneath the muslin the red became pink, and this delicate shading was repeated in the window curtains, which were of Indian muslin lined with pink silk and ornamented with a fringe of black and lilac.

"At equal distances on the wall above the divan were six sockets of silver-gilt, each of which supported two candles, while from the centre of the ceiling hung a highly polished lustre of the same material.

"The carpet was like a camel's-hair shawl, and seemed a mute reminder of the poetry of Persia. The furniture was covered with white cashmere relieved by lilac and black. The clock and candelabras were of gold and marble. The one table which the boudoir contained was covered with white cashmere, while all about were jardinières of white and red roses."

Behind the semicircle was a secret passage, at one end of which was an iron cot and at the other a desk; and here it was that Balzac, secure from intrusion, worked and composed at his ease.

To return, however, to the Widow Durand. In 1838 he wrote to Madame Hanska, the lady who subsequently became his wife:—

"The Widow Durand is dead. She was killed by the contemptible conduct of the daily papers, who have betrayed a secret which should have been sacred to every man of honor."

After this misfortune Balzac installed himself openly at Les Jardies, a country house which he had built at Ville d'Avray, and where he was, as he expressed it, "like the lantern of Demosthenes, and not, as every one else says, of Diogenes;" but when, a year or two later, he took up his residence in the Rue Basse, at Passy he surrounded himself with all his former precautions, instituted a series of countersigns which he changed weekly, and transformed himself into "Madame Bri...."

When guarded in this way from any intrusion, Balzac would work from twelve to twenty-one hours a day. His usual hours of sleep were from six in the evening until midnight. Then he would bathe, don the white robe of a Dominican friar, poise a black skull cap on his head, and, under the influence of coffee and by the light of a dozen candles, would work incessantly till he could work no more.

His work completed, the lion would forsake his den, and for an evening or two he would be seen in the Loge Infernale at the opera, invariably carrying a massive cane whose head glittered with jewels, and which Madame de Girardin was pleased to imagine rendered him invisible at will;[11] or he would make brief apparitions in the salons of the literati and nobility, and then, suddenly, without a word of warning, he would shut himself up as impenetrably as before.

His manner of writing was stamped with the same eccentricity which characterized all his habits. When a subject which he proposed to treat had been well

[11] See *La Canne de M. de Balzac*, par Madame de Girardin. Dumont, 1838.

considered, he would cover thirty or forty sheets with a scaffolding of ideas and phrases, which he then sent off to the printer, who returned them in columns wired and centred on large placards. The work, freed in this way from any personality and its errors at once apparent, was then strengthened and corrected. On a second reading the forty pages grew to a hundred, two hundred on the third, and so on, while on the proof-sheets themselves new lines would start from the beginning, the middle, or the end of a phrase; and if the margins were insufficient, other sheets of paper were pinned or glued to the placards, which were again and again returned, corrected, and reprinted, until the work was at last satisfactorily completed.

But perhaps the most graphic description of Balzac's manner of writing is the one contained in an article by Edouard Ourliac in the "Figaro" for the 15th of December, 1837, of which the following is a free translation:—

THE MISFORTUNES AND ADVENTURES OF CÉSAR BIROTTEAU BEFORE HIS BIRTH.

Let us sing, drink, and embrace, like the chorus in an opéra bouffe; let us waft kisses in the air and turn on our toes, as they do in the ballet.

Let us rejoice now that we may. The "Figaro," without appearing to have done so, has conquered the elements, all the malefactors, and every sublunary cataclysm.

The "Figaro" has conquered César Birotteau.

Never did the angered gods, never did Juno, Neptune, M. de Rambuteau, or the prefect of the police, oppose against Jason, Theseus, or the wayfarers of the capital, greater obstacles, monsters, ruins, dragons, demolitions, than these two unhappy octavos. We have them at last, and we know their cost.

The public will have but the trouble to read them, though that should count as a pleasure.

As to M. de Balzac, twenty days of labor, two reams of paper, another masterpiece, that counts as nothing.

Whatever else it may be considered, it is at least a typographical exploit and a worthy example of literary and commercial heroism.

Writer, publisher, and printer, all deserve the praise of their countrymen.

Posterity will gossip about the binders, and our grand-nephews will regret that they do not know the names of the apprentices.

I regret it myself,—otherwise I would tell them.

The "Figaro" promised the book for the 15th of December,

and M. de Balzac began it on the 17th of November.

M. de Balzac and the "Figaro" have the singular habit of keeping their word.

The printing-press was prepared, and pawed the ground like an excited charger.

M. de Balzac sent immediately two hundred sheets, scribbled in five nights of fever.

Every one knows how he writes. It was an outline, a chaos, an apocalypse, a Hindu poem.

The office paled. The time was short, the writing unheard of. The monster was transformed and translated as nearly as possible into familiar signs. No one could make head or tail of it. Back it went to the author. The author sent back the first two proofs glued on enormous placards.

It was frightful, it was pitiful. From each sign, from each printed word, shot a penstroke, gleaming and gliding like a sky-rocket, and bursting at the extremity in a luminous fire of phrases, epithets, substantives, underlined, crossed, intermingled, erased, and superposed. Its aspect was simply dazzling.

Fancy four or five hundred arabesques of this kind, interlacing, knotted together, climbing and slipping from one margin to another and from the bottom to the top.

Fancy twelve geographical maps entangling cities, rivers, and mountains in the same confusion, a skein harassed by a cat, all the hieroglyphics of the Pharonian dynasty, or twenty fireworks exploding at once.

The office then was far from gay. The typesetters beat their breasts, the presses groaned, the proof-readers tore their hair and the apprentices became howling idiots. The most intelligent recognized the Persian alphabet, others the Madagascan, while one or two considered them to be the symbolic characters of Vishnu.

They worked on chance and by the grace of God.

The next day M. de Balzac sent back two pages of the purest Chinese. It was then the 1st of December. A generous typesetter offered to blow out his brains. Then other sheets were brought, written in the most legible Siamese. Three compositors lost their sight and the little French that they knew.

The proofs were sent back seven consecutive times; then, a few symptoms of excellent French appeared, and there was even noticed a certain connection between the phrases; but the day was fast approaching, and we felt that the book would never appear.

Desolation was at its height, and it was at this point that the work became further complicated by an admirable concourse of calamities.

At the time when haste was the greatest, the miserable being who that night carried the proof-sheets to M. de Balzac was waylaid and robbed.

M. de Balzac had had the forethought to establish himself at Chaillot. The miserable being screamed and yelled. The bandits took to their heels. One proof-sheet was found at Neuilly, another in an orchard, a third descending the Seine. It is certain that they were thrown away only on account of their illegibility. Misfortune has its advantages.

The proofs were recovered, but the night was lost. There were cries and gnashing of teeth. The end was fast approaching. However, the typesetters took courage and the workmen took the bit in their teeth. The office galloped. The compositors foamed at the mouth, the presses ravened, the binders were on springs, the apprentices danced with excitement, the proof-reader shook like an epileptic, and the foreman had convulsions. The office was a cage of palsied lunatics.

The work was again taken in hand, and M. de Balzac and the "Figaro" have kept their word.

"César Birotteau" will see the light of day on the 15th of December. We have it now, and we hold it tight. The office is armed, insured, and barricaded. Smoking is not permitted. There are lightning-rods on the roof, and mounted guards at the door.

Every precaution has been taken against accidents and the ardor of our subscribers.

At this moment "César Birotteau" is a work in two volumes, an immense tableau, an entire poem, composed, written, and corrected fifteen times by M. de Balzac in twenty days, and deciphered, disentangled, and reprinted fifteen times in the same period. It may be added that M. de Balzac kept forty other workmen busy with something else at another office.

We will not now consider the value of the work.

It may be everything, or but a masterpiece.

The names of Balzac's characters are all taken from real life; for, like Dickens, his theory was that names which were invented gave no life to imaginary creations, and, as did the English novelist, he gathered many of them from the signboards in the street. His joy at the discovery of Matifat was almost as great as his delight in finding Cardot. He found the former in the Rue de la Perle, in the Marais. "I can see him now," he said; "he will have the pallid face of a cat. But Cardot is different: he will be dry as a bone, hasty and ill-tempered."

In 1840, Balzac proposed to write for the "Revue Parisienne"—a periodical which, it may be explained, appeared but three times, and whose three numbers Balzac wrote entirely—the story of a man of genius, who, used as a tool by others, died through the ingratitude of those whom he had raised to magnificent positions, and who had then abandoned him to poverty and want.

Such a character needed a name proportioned to his destiny; a name which explained and announced him as clearly as the cannon-ball announces the cannon; a name which would be peculiarly his own, and would reflect his face, his figure, his voice, his past, his future, his genius, his passions, his misfortunes, and his glory.

But this supernatural alliance of man and name was not immediately discoverable, and Balzac, who had put into circulation as many cognomens as are contained in the "Almanach de Gotha," expressed himself incapable of manufacturing it. A name, he considered, could no more be fabricated than could granite or marble. They were all three the work of time and revolutions. They made themselves.

As a last and supreme resource, therefore, he set out one day, in company with Léon Gozlan, on a journey, in search of a baptismal signboard for his hero; and from the Barrière de l'Étoile to the summits of Montmartre they zigzagged across Paris, subjecting every name they encountered to the closest scrutiny.

Thousands of names were examined, analyzed, and rejected, until at last Gozlan, utterly worn out, refused to walk another step.

Balzac looked at him, it is to be supposed, very much as Columbus looked at his mutinous sailors, and by force of entreaties obtained, not three days' grace, but three streets more.

In the first two nothing was found, but at the extremity of the third Balzac suddenly changed color, and cried in a voice broken by emotion,—

"There, there! Read that name!"

Above a narrow, oblong door, which opened on a sombre courtyard, there hung a sign which bore for device the name of Marcas.

"Our journey is at an end!" Balzac exclaimed; "it terminates in a blaze of glory. The name of my hero shall be Marcas. Marcas contains the philosopher, the statesman, and the poet. I will call him Z. Marcas, and thereby add to his name a flame, a tiara, and a star. Nothing could be better. I wonder, however, who this Marcas is; surely some great artist."

"He is a tailor," Gozlan brutally replied; "there is another sign of his in the courtyard."

Balzac looked deeply chagrined.

"No matter," he said; "he merited a better fate. If I seem annoyed, it is not that I am lacking in respect for tailors in general, but because his calling reminds me of certain debts and a few protested notes."

A day or two later the "Revue Parisienne" appeared, and with it the story of Z. Marcas, now forming part of the "Scènes de la Vie Politique" and containing the following monograph:—

"A certain harmony existed between the man and the name. This Z. with which Marcas was preceded, which was to be seen on the address of his letters, and with which he always completed his signature,—this last letter of the alphabet presented to the imagination a something which was indescribably fatal.

"Marcas! Repeat over to yourself this name, composed of two syllables: does it not seem to contain a sinister significance? does it not seem as though its owner were born to be martyred.

"Though weird and wild, this name has nevertheless the right to descend to posterity: it is well composed, it is easily pronounced, and possesses the brevity required of famous names. Is it not as soft as it is bizarre? but does it not also seem unfinished?

"I would not dare to affirm that destiny is uninfluenced by a name, for between the deeds of men and their names there are inexplicable affinities and visible discords which at once astonish and surprise. But this subject will some day assuredly form part of the occult sciences.

"Does not the Z. present a thwarted and contradicted appearance? does it not represent the contingent and fantastic zigzags of a tormented life? What ill wind can have blown on this letter that in every language to which it is admitted commands barely fifty words! Marcas' Christian name was Zépherin. Saint Zépherin is highly venerated in Brittany. Marcas was a Breton.

"Examine the name again. Z. Marcas! The entire existence of the man is contained in the fantastic assemblage of these seven letters. Seven!—the most significant of the cabalistic numbers. Marcas died at the age of thirty-five; his life therefore was composed of but seven lustres. Marcas! Does not the sound bring to you the idea of something precious, broken in a noiseless fall?"

The fatality which Balzac conceived as attaching to Marcas was by no means limited to this imaginary creation. It followed him into real life, and was at one time a source of such serious preoccupation that he stood one evening for two hours in the square of the Château d'Eau confidently awaiting some fortunate occurrence, and like Gautier in "Mademoiselle de Maupin" he awoke on certain days in a state of great agitation, trembling at every noise, and convinced that the happiness of his life was somehow at stake.

These extraordinary sensations naturally led to a belief in the supernatural; and as his mother, who was also interested in the abnormal, was acquainted with all the celebrated mesmerists and mediums of the day, he was readily furnished with opportunities of experimenting in magnetism and clairvoyance. His charming story of "Ursule Mirouët" unquestionably proves that he subsequently became a firm believer in that occult electricity which is variously known as the Theopœa of the ancients, the Akâsa of the modern Hindu, and the psychic force of Sergeant Cox; while his account of the soul-projection of "Séraphita" is vivid enough to satisfy the most exacting hierophant, and would have passed him, initiate, into the brotherhood of the Theosophists.

But perhaps the most curious evidence of his every-day faith in divination is that contained in the two following extracts from his correspondence:—

TO M. CHAPELAIN, PHYSICIAN.

Paris, *May, 1832.*

Sir,—I am attracted by the power of somnambulism, and wonder why you have not sought to obtain from some lucid subject the causes of this disaster.[12]

Science is interested therein, and its discovery would be an eternal honor to us.

Had I not been ill for a week past I would have ascended to the honors of practice, and endeavored to convince myself whether the power of a somnambulist was limited or infinite.

The second extract is from a letter addressed to his mother a year later:—

"I send you herewith two pieces of flannel which I have worn on the body. Take them to M. Chapelain, and when he has examined the first, ask of him the cause and position of the malady[13] and how it should be treated. See that everything is clearly explained. Then with the second piece ask the why and wherefore of the blister ordered in the precedent consultation.

"Be careful to keep the flannels well wrapped up, that the emanations may not be disturbed."

Balzac's hatred of journalists was intense, and from Sainte-Beuve down to the most insignificant penny-a-liner all were enveloped in the same superb contempt.

No branch of the profession was exempt from this antipathy, and critics and *feuilletonistes* shared alike in his wholesale condemnation:—

"They want my scalp, do they, these Mohicans of the press! Bah! I will drink out of their skulls."

Drink he did, indeed, and long delicious draughts, at that; and in picking up with the point of his pen the venality, envy, and petty spites of the trade, he drew in the "Illusions Perdues," in which Jules Janin figures in the transparent disguise of Étienne Lousteau, a picture of journalism which was as faithfully unpleasant as it was pitying and contemptuous. In this respect, however, it is well to state that no one was as indifferent to the opinion of the press as Balzac himself. He rarely, if ever, read the criticisms on his books, and left them, in the consciousness of their worth, to find their level unaided.

One of the causes of his disdain of everything which smacked of journalism was this: He had engaged to write "Séraphita" for the "Revue des Deux Mondes," and shortly after the story had been delivered he learned that it was published at St. Petersburg. Thinking, as was but natural, that the editor had been the victim of some audacious theft, he hastened to tell him what he had heard; and his astonishment may be readily imagined when he was informed that the Russian edition

[12] The cholera.
[13] Stomachic disorders, caused by the abuse of coffee.

had appeared with the sanction of the editor himself, who not only insisted that he had a perfect right to do as he pleased with the manuscript, but positively refused to make any indemnity. Thereupon, Balzac, in spite of the remonstrances of his friends, who pointed out that any contest with the "Revue," whose word was law, would inevitably result in the closing of its columns to him, began a lawsuit, alleging that, independent of the pecuniary loss which he suffered, a precedent of this kind, once established, would in the future be highly prejudicial, not only to him, but to all his confrères. Much to his amazement, however, the defendant appeared in court with a list of signatures of almost all of those whom he had sought to defend at his own risk and peril, who attested that from a literary as well as from an ethical standpoint they considered the action of the editor of the "Revue des Deux Mondes" as eminently right and proper.

The law was, none the less, perfectly clear. Balzac won the suit, and with it a host of enemies, whose hatred was so vigorous that it barely abated, even after his death. Their insults delighted him. "Fire away," he would say; "the armor is strong. Your abuse is an advertisement; your praise would lull the public to sleep, but your diatribes wake them up. Besides, you hit the mark sometimes, and every fault you signalize I correct, which in the end is so much gained."

Among the host of enemies thus aroused were those who, not content with denying his genius, advanced their artillery into private life, and painted him in the possession of every vice in the criminal statutes; and it is from the falsehoods of these guerrilleros that all the stupidities which have been told concerning him found their primal gestation. Not only his morality, his honesty, his sobriety, were attacked, but even his name was denied to him. The *de* was declared not only an affectation, but a theft; and when some one said to him, in allusion thereto, "But you are no connection of the De Balzac d'Entragues," "Ah! am I not?" he answered placidly. "Well, then, so much the worse for them."

CHAPTER II.

THE COMÉDIE HUMAINE.

"One would say he had read the inscription on the gates of Busyrane, — 'Be bold;' and on the second gate, — 'Be bold, be bold, and evermore be bold;' and then again had paused well at the third gate, — 'Be not too bold.'" — EMERSON, *Plato*.

The general plan and outline of the "Comédie Humaine" originated in a comparison between humanity and animal existence. That which Buffon had achieved in zoölogy, Balzac proposed to accomplish in moral science, and the habits and customs as well as the vices and virtues of his contemporaries found in him a secretary whose inventory offers to posterity an elaborate insight into the every-day life of France in the nineteenth century, and realizes for their future curiosity that work which the ancient monarchies have neglected to bequeath to us as their own civilizations.

But the pictures of two or three thousand of the most striking figures of an epoch required, in a general history of society, not only frames but galleries, and the work therefore is divided into,

Scènes de la Vie Privée.
Scènes de la Vie de Province.
Scènes de la Vie Parisienne.
Scènes de la Vie Politique.
Scènes de la Vie Militaire.
Scènes de la Vie de Campagne.

These six subdivisions are grouped under the general title of "Études de Mœurs," and in them the attempt has been made to examine and explain the general causes of earthly happiness and misery, as demonstrated in the results obtainable in the practice of the great principles of order and mortality, or in the selfish abandonment to purely personal interests.

Happiness, Balzac considered, consisted in the exercise of our faculties as applied to realities. But inasmuch as its principles vary with each latitude, and ideas of right and wrong find their modifications in the climate, he concluded that morals and convictions were valueless terms, and that happiness was to be found, first, in violent emotions which undermine existence; second, in regular occupations functionating like mechanism; or, lastly, in the study of the laws of nature and in the application of the lessons thereby derived.

In his treatment of this subject he has prepared a complete history of the effects of the agitation of social existence, and each of the foregoing divisions represents a particular aspect of life.

In the "Scènes de la Vie Privée," life is represented between the last developments of childhood and the first calculations of virility. These scenes contain tableaux of the emotions and undefined sensations combined with pictures of the errors committed through ignorance of the exigencies of the world.

The "Scènes de la Vie de Province" represents that phase of existence in which passions, calculations, and ideas take the place of sensations, impulses, and illusions. The instincts of the young man of twenty are generous; at thirty he calculates and turns egotist. These scenes therefore initiate the reader into the thousand aspects of the transition through which a man passes when abandoning the thoughtless impulses of adolescence for the politic attitudes of manhood. Life becomes serious: positive interests jostle with violent passions, disillusions begin, the social machinery is revealed, and from the shock of moral or pecuniary interests the crime bursts in the midst of the most tranquil household.

Herein are unveiled the petty annoyances by whose periodicity a poignant interest is concentrated in the slightest detail of existence. Herein are also exposed the petty rivalries, the jealousies born of vicinage, and the family worries, whose increasing force degrades and weakens the most resolute will. The charm of dreams escapes; the prosaic and the matter of fact alone exist; woman reasons, and no longer feels; she calculates where before she gave. Life is now ripened and shaded.

In the "Scènes de la Vie Parisienne" the questions are enlarged, and existence painted in bold outlines gradually arrives at the frontiers of decrepitude. Herein purity of sentiment is exceptional: it is broken in the play of interests and scattered by the mechanism of the world. Virtue is calumniated, innocence is purchased. Passions become vices, emotions ruinous gratifications; everything is analyzed, bought, and sold. Life is a bazaar; humanity has but two forms, that of the deceiver and the deceived; it is a struggle and a combat, and the victor is he who best throttles society and moulds it to his own ends. The death of relatives is awaited; the honest man is a simpleton; generosity is a means, religion a governmental necessity, probity a policy; everything is marketable; absurdity is an advertisement, ridicule a passport, and youth, which has lived a hundred years, insults old age.

These scenes close the tableaux of individual existence, and their three frameworks contain representations of youth, manhood, and old age. First the bloom of life, the expansion of the soul, and the radiance of love; then come the calculations, the transformation of affection into passion; and, lastly, the accumulation of interests and the continual satisfaction of the senses joined to the inevitable weariness of mind and body.

Nothing but that which affects the individual proper has herein been treated, and the fragments of the "Scènes de la Vie Politique" express, in consequence, a wider range of thought. In these pages the actors represent the interest of the masses, and place themselves above those laws to which the types in the preced-

ing series were subjected. The foregoing divisions described the constant antago-
nism of thought and sentiment, but in these scenes thought is an organizing force
and sentiment is completely abolished. They are, however, incomplete, as are also
the "Scènes de la Vie Militaire," in which Balzac proposed to represent the action
as taking place, not in an apartment, but on the battle-field; not in the struggle of
man with man, but in the concussion of France and Europe, in the slaughter of the
conquered and the pæans of the victors.

After these pages, whose completion was prevented by his sudden death, the
calm and peaceful pictures of the "Scènes de la Vie de Campagne" follow in orderly sequence. They represent rest after exertion, landscapes after interiors, the hush
of the country after the uproar of the city, the cicatrice after the wound. This last
division contains the same interests and the same struggles, but weakened now
by lack of contact, like passions grown dull in solitude. It is the twilight of a busy
day, a summer evening solemn with sombre shadows. It contains the purest characters and the application of the great principles of order, morality, and religion,
and its actors, worn with the fatigues of the world, mingle complacently with the
innocence of childhood.[14]

Thus completed, the entire work has its geography and its own genealogy,
its localities and their concomitants, its personages and their deeds. It has its own
armorial, its nobility and middle class, its artisans, its peasants, and its army. It
is a world in itself. But its most striking feature is the admirable unity preserved
throughout; and this unity is undoubtedly due to a suggestion derived from the
works of Sir Walter Scott, whom Balzac considered as a gifted sculptor who chis-
eled magnificent figures and draped them with genius and sublimity, but, while
presenting the seductive effects of a marvelous analysis, left them lacking in syn-
thesis and totally unrelated.

"The Waverley Novels," he said,[15] "resemble the Musée de la Rue des Pe-
tits-Augustins, in which each object, while magnificent in design, relates but to
itself. Genius is complete only when to the faculty of creating it joins the power of coördinating its creations. The gifts of observation and description are in
themselves insufficient; they must tend to a certain result. The Scotch bard was
possessed of too clear a vision not to have understood this axiom, but its understanding assuredly came too late." To this reflection the unity of the "Comédie
Humaine" is probably due; and that it may not be objected that certain of its pas-
sages are unrelated to the others, it is well to note that Balzac died too suddenly
to be able to connect the broken threads, which in any event are but few and far
between.

But the task of rendering his work at once interesting and instructive was
one of much greater difficulty than that of Scott's, who drew his characters from
former days, when every class of society was clearly defined, and clothed them
from a wardrobe opulent with historical effects; whereas Balzac was obliged to
offer in clear relief the almost imperceptible differences of the types of yesterday
and to-day, that through an equality of fortune and education have destroyed the

---

[14] See Introduction by M. Felix Davin to the first edition of the *Comédie Humaine*.
[15] *Correspondance de H. de Balzac.*

contrasts which once existed between the different degrees of the social order. Aided, however, by that peculiar intuition which never forsook him, he chose from among the physiognomies of his epoch an assortment of those fugitive traits which are imperceptible to the eyes of the vulgar; and in scrutinizing face after face, attentive to the changes of expression and inflections of voice, he was enabled to present a series of individualities which are far more realistic than those of his illustrious predecessor.

After displaying in the "Études de Mœurs" all the moral and physical transformations through which mankind passes, and after describing the social effects of their natural or civil positions, Balzac sought in the "Études Philosophiques" to demonstrate the causes of these effects; and while the first part of the "Comédie Humaine" contains but a series of individualities typified in the treatment of his subject, in the second part are to be found the same types individualized: as, for example, where in the "Études de Mœurs" Grandet is purely and simply a miser, avarice in the "Études Philosophiques" is incarnated in the person of Maître Cornélius, and the subject, like a sponge, gains in weight what it loses in breadth.

The "Études Philosophiques" is the fruit of analyzed comparisons of all the works which the philosophers of antiquity and the specialists of his day had produced on the intellect; and starting with the famous axiom of Jean Jacques Rousseau, that "l'homme qui pense est un animal dépravé," —an idea which, as is well known, found its poetic interpretation in Byron's "Manfred," and its dramatic aspect in the "Faust" of Goethe, —Balzac proceeds to prove that ideas and sentiments are simply dissolvents of a greater or less activity; and taking as his premises the admitted fact that instincts violently excited by factitious or fortuitous circumstances produce unconsciousness and even death, and also that thought, when augmented by the transitory force of passion, may become a poison or a dagger, he infers, from the ravages produced by the intellect, that thought is the most active agent in the disorganization of man, and consequently of society. "Consider," he says in "Louis Lambert," "the difference between man who desires nothing and lives like a plant for a hundred years, and the creating artist who suffers early death. Where the sun is, there is thought and brevity of existence; where the cold is, there is torpor and longevity." Then, after considering man as a simple organization, he brandishes the proposition that vitality decreases in exact proportion to the strength of desire and the dissipation of thought, and leads the reader, therewith, through the gradual development of his theory, which is first attacked in "La Peau de Chagrin." This weird and fantastic production, in which skepticism and the supernatural join hands, represents the ravages of thought and the supreme expression of egotism as seared by the hot iron of civilization.

In "La Recherche de l'Absolu," the theme is continued, but viewed in a broader and more comprehensive light. In "La Peau de Chagrin," the individual is destroyed by the force of desire. In "La Recherche de l'Absolu," the pursuit of an idea annihilates an entire family. The first is the world of pleasure, an epoch in itself; the second is the world of science, and glitters with brilliant hypotheses. In both instances, an idea, gradually strengthened, becomes a passion and a disorganizing force. In "L'Adieu," happiness, exalted to the highest degree, becomes a destructive agency. In "Le Réquisitionnaire", a mother is killed by the violence of maternal affection. In "El Verdugo," a father is slain by his son that a title may be preserved. In "Le Drame au Bord de la Mer," a son is slain by his father that an hereditary instinct may be destroyed. In "Maître Cornélius," avarice kills the miser. In "Le Chef d'Œuvre Inconnu," art kills the artist. In "Gambara," the composer is crazed by his own conceptions. In "L'Enfant Maudit," terror is the destroyer, and the subject treated herein finds a natural and logical sequence in the "Auberge Rouge." In "Les Proscrits," the sentiment of religion becomes the destroyer, and in "Séraphita" the same idea is more vividly presented. "César Birotteau," an existence untroubled by misery, is, through sudden good fortune, cut off as by a scythe. In the "Église," the agent is incredulity, but in "Louis Lambert" is to be found the most severe deduction from the fundamental proposition in that it represents the thinker killed by thought.

The destructive power of the mind and imagination, from the Neronian conflagration to the suicide of Castlereagh and Chatterton, the aphasia of Emerson, and the insanity of Tourgénieff, is too well known and too thoroughly understood to need further commentary in these pages; and in connection with this it need but be said that, while the attraction of gravity had been witnessed by countless generations, as it remained to Newton to formulate the obvious propositions of cause and effect, so in this branch of mental science, whose results have been patent since the beginning of history, a Balzac was necessary for the full elucidation of the subject, and for the proper presentation of the conclusions derived from the psycho-mental evidence of ages.

After having, in the "Études de Mœurs," described society in every aspect, and demonstrated in the "Études Philosophiques" all the underlying causes of the general results, Balzac proposed in the third and last division of the "Comédie Humaine," namely, in the "Études Analytiques," to examine the principles upon which the first two rest.

This last division, however, is one of the few unfinished windows of his Aladdin's palace, for, out of the six volumes which it was to contain, two only were written before death intervened. These two works, the "Physiologie du Mariage" and the "Petites Misères de la Vie Conjugale," are a series of duos between husband and wife, augmented at times by the tenor notes of the *amant*. The first is dedicated to the reader, and contains the deceptions of the husband; the second, those of the wife. At once malicious and diabolically witty, these two books are as delicately analytical as the deductions of Leuwenhoeck and Swammerdam, and abound with that peculiar though refreshing condiment which is generally known as Gallic salt.

It is to be regretted that these two books, the first of which was published at the outset of the author's career, and the second towards the close of his life, were not strengthened and augmented by the others with which he proposed to accompany them, and whose subjects and titles—namely, "Anatomie des Corps Enseignants," "Pathologie de la Vie Sociale," "Monographie de la Vertu," "Dialogue Philosophique et Politique sur la Perfection du XIXe Siècle"—have alone descended to us; for this vein of literary treasure can never be profitably worked save by another Balzac or a modern Aristophanes.

It was in 1844 that Balzac said, "The first half of the present century will be found to have been greatly influenced by four men,—Napoleon, Cuvier, O'Connell, and myself. The first lived on the blood of Europe, the second espoused the globe, the third became the incarnation of an entire race, while I shall have carried a complete society in my brain."

Though almost another half century has now elapsed since these words were uttered, it would seem that the influence which he was then conscious of exerting is even more vigorous than before. The characters which he painted formed, it is true, part of a Paris now dead and forgotten, but the types have survived, and the lessons which he deduced therefrom are as eminently instructive now as they were in the days when he wrote; and while, taking the world at large as the groundwork of his edifice, man was necessarily but the detail, he has, in his description thereof, painted him in every phase,—consequent and inconsequent, neither completely good nor completely vicious, logical at times, and sometimes great, but incessantly opposing his own interests to the laws of society in that gigantic struggle of customs and sentiments which is as inconsistent to-day as it was fifty years ago.

When the "fiat lux" was pronounced, and man completed, Balzac turned to his natural companion, and in his portraiture of woman not a single type is lacking. Herein he is unexcelled and unsurpassable. That which Euripides considered as the most terrible of all misfortunes, and De Maistre nothing but a beautiful animal, found its most graphic expression through him. As a faithful naturalist, he has, in descending the spiral of civilization, described and classified the *femina simplex;* but the ideal woman, sublime in her errors, magnificent in her devotion, and royal in her forgiveness, has found her geographer in him. His descriptions of Madame de Beauséant, the Duchesse de Langeais, Madame Firmiani, the Countess in "Colonel Chabert," Madame Claës, Madame Jules, Madame de Montsauf, Béatrix, and Mademoiselle des Touches comprise woman almost in her entirety; they are landmarks in psychological study; and so true to nature are they that their appearance marked a new era in literature.

It is in these portraits that Balzac is most realistic; and while a few of the most admirable among them are sometimes erring, yet it will be admitted that womankind is not composed exclusively of angels; perfection is often dull, and a fault may be a virtue. By way of contrast, however, he has, in Eugénie Grandet, Madame Firmiani, Madame de la Chanterie, Marguerite Claës, Madame Jules, Agathe Rouget, Pierrette, Madame Hulot, and Ursule Mirouët, not only solved the difficult problem of rendering virtue interesting, but he has created in frames of impeccable beauty a series of irreproachable Madonnas.

His revelation of woman is completed in a special and parallel study of love. Love he considered the mainspring of humanity; without it, religion, history, romance, and art would be useless; and he has analyzed, dissected, and explained its every phase, hesitation, palpitation, and tenderness.

Beyond the scenic effects which he lent to passion, Balzac entered thoroughly into the specialties of trade and profession, and it seems almost incredible that one mind could have grappled with the details of the practice of law which are so admirably described in the "Contrat de Mariage," in his portrait of Derville the lawyer, Peerquin the notary, and the proceedings in "César Birotteau," while imagining such types as Vautrin, who dominated Paris from the depths of the galleys, or La Fille aux yeux d'or languishing in her octagonal boudoir.

As Bianchou he is alienist and physician; in Dr. Mirouët he is medium and mesmerist; he is a miser in Grandet and discounter in Gobseck; he is vicar at Tours and old maid at Issoudun. None better than he has described that class of fascinating scoundrels of which Rastignac is the type, nor painted more clearly the heralds of *ennui* and philosophers of satiety than he has done in De Marsay and Maxime de Trailles. In "Les Deux Poètes" he is printer and manufacturer of paper; in the "Cousin Pons" he presents the flower of an imagination intoxicated with the master paintings of great artists; while in the "Illusions Perdues" the journalist is dissected and the publisher decomposed.

In the veins of his characters there is not a drop of ink; they live, move, and have their being, and their eyelashes are as delicately finished as their epigrams.

Starting from the mud and vermin of Parisian by-ways, and ascending to the steps of the throne, Balzac garnered every possible type, no two of which are similar; each is original and all are profoundly human; and while the dregs of London are not further removed from the splendors of Teheran than is mother Nourrison from the Duc de Grandlieu, yet Balzac's intuition divined the one as clearly as he described the other.

In his transitions and contrasts, however, there is as little abruptness as there is in the marriage of the blue of the skies with the green of a landscape; changes follow in orderly and natural sequence, and the mind of the reader is only confused at the multiplicity of his attainments, which present in turn houses and costumes, interiors and countries, intermingled with plot, science, religion, politics, agriculture, erudition, mysticism, and wit.

Balzac was also a delicious landscape painter, and his scenes from Brittany in "Les Chouans," his landscapes of Touraine and particularly that of Vouvay in "La Femme de Trente Ans," the grand sketch of Norway in "Séraphita," that of the Mediterranean island in "La Duchesse de Langeais," are cited by Davin as masterpieces of graphic description.

The resources of Balzac's genius are perhaps as clearly exhibited in "Eugénie Grandet" as in any of his other works, and the appearance of this romance gave the keynote to the present Realistic school. "Eugénie Grandet" is the conquest of absolute truth in art. It is the drama applied to the most simple events of life; the fusion of the trivial and the sublime, the pathetic and the grotesque. It is a picture of life as it is, and the model of what a novel should be.

The *motif* here commenced is admirably continued in "Le Curé de Tours," which contains none of those elements heretofore considered indispensable in the manufacture of fiction. From these pages love and marriage are banished; there is barely an event to be mentioned, yet the dumb, tortuous struggle between the two priests is at once clear cut and peculiarly vivid. Herein the most humble trivialities of the subject are elevated and dramatized, and to attentive eyes this book will perhaps contain the secret of Balzac's superiority; for as no rôle is poor to a good actor, Balzac in this story demonstrates that nothing was small beneath his pen.

The interiors of Gerard Dow, with their vast chimneys lit by flickering flames, their polished floors, walls hung with tapestries, their sculptured cornices and quaint and curious furniture, their shadowed backgrounds and doors which seem about to open upon some mysterious room, are to be found in "La Recherche de l'Absolu," in which the opulent detail of the Flemish school is equaled, if not surpassed. Here, as in "Eugénie Grandet," the drama is formed of the fusion of the trivial and the sublime, and for the proper presentation of the subject he extracted from the past of chemistry its possibilities for the future.

This work, as is the case with almost all his others, contains evidence of the most obstinate researches; and in this respect it may be noted that the majority of his books are the result of patient labor and prolonged meditations.

"Ursule Mirouët," one of his most chaste conceptions, is the fruit of exhaustive experiments in clairvoyance. "Séraphita" was born of the suggestions of a hundred works of the mystics. "César Birotteau" is a text-book on bankruptcy.

The production of "Gambara" and "Massimillia Doni" necessitated not only a thorough musical schooling, but vast operatic knowledge, and before attacking his subject Balzac engaged a violinist to saturate him with Rossini. "La Grande Bretèche" is the essence of the Causes Célèbres, and dowered French literature with a new shudder. The "Contrat de Mariage" is a code of legal *finesse.*

"Maître Cornélius," which with the exception of "Catherine de Médicis" contains the only ghosts that he has evoked from the night of the past, is an attempt to rehabilitate Louis XI., and to refute the historical portion of "Quentin Durward."

"Les Deux Proscrits" was the result of prolonged meditations on the works of Dante, while "La Dernière Incarnation de Vautrin" is a dictionary of prison slang.

But the works for which he cared the most and on which he expended the greatest amount of labor were "Louis Lambert" and "Le Médecin de Campagne."

In "Louis Lambert," he asks whether electricity is not the basis of the particular fluid from which ideas are derived, and proceeds thereupon to consider thought as a complete system similar to that of vegetation; and after analyzing the birth, life, or death of certain thoughts,[16] he expresses the opinion that ideas and sentiments are endowed with physical properties, such as weight and movement; and after fortifying it with striking examples of expectation, fear, anger, and determination, he concludes that facts do not exist, that ideas alone endure, and that volition is a material force, similar to that of steam.

In spite of the amount of labor which a work of this kind necessitated, a still greater amount was expended on "Le Médecin de Campagne," of which every line and every phrase was weighed, rewritten, and corrected again and again. In this work he attempted to grasp the simple beauty of the Scriptures, to surpass the "Vicar of Wakefield," and to put the "Imitation of Christ" into action; but its pages

---

[16] See also *La Peau de Chagrin.*

were written above the level of the ordinary reader, and in spite of its profundity of thought it is perhaps the least known of all his writings.

The romance, however, which gained for him the greatest favor in the boudoirs of Europe was the "Mémoires de Deux Jeunes Mariées," which is one of the few works in which happy and satisfied love has been successfully depicted. In Rousseau there was too much rhetoric, in Richardson too much pretension; Scott was hampered by English prudery, and is consequently chill as an icicle; the poets as a rule were too extravagant and too much engrossed in metaphors; and it remained to Balzac to describe the insensate fears and unreasoning jealousies of that passion of which many speak, but few have known.

The masterful handling of these widely contrasting subjects shows not only an equipment of profound penetration and power of observation, but also an erudition at once varied and luminous. His works are those of an anatomist from whom nothing escaped, a psychologist from whom nothing was hidden, and a realist who described all. Joined thereto was the gift of adjective: in this he is the Benvenuto Cellini of literature, for his words seem less like symbols of speech than awakeners of trains of thought.

His originality is entirely undisputed. It would not be a difficult task to point out the buried hands which modeled the grandiose figure of Hugo, and the tombs ransacked by Shakespeare are still open to inspection; but Balzac was totally without literary ancestry. The influence of Scott and Hoffmann, at that time enormous, possibly presided at the conception of some of his earlier works, and brought to them strength from the massiveness of the one and coloring from the unexpectedness of the other; they were perhaps the transitory models of a necessary apprenticeship, in which the masters were soon to be neglected and surpassed. Aside from this early schooling, Balzac is indebted to no one,—neither to the Greeks nor to the Romans, to the Italian school, to the Trouvères of feudal France nor to the Minnesingers of the Middle Ages; and even where Hoffmann is not, he at least is entirely modern and absolutely original; for the fantastic effects of the former were drawn from Micromegas, who had already extracted them from Cyrano de Bergerac,—a well into which, it may be noted, Voltaire himself has dipped; and in this respect, that it may not be objected that the "Contes Drolatiques" are but a continuation of Rabelais, Béroalde de Verville, and the Reine de Navarre, it is well to point out that where but the female was seen by these writers Balzac discovered the woman, a difference surely as great as between the bottle and the wine.

And here perhaps a word may be said in regard to the present Realistic school, of which he was the founder, and whose influence is daily becoming more noticeable and apparent.

The term *present* Realistic school is used advisedly; for though it was only about twenty-five or thirty years ago that realism began to be seriously considered, it is erroneous to suppose that it is of purely modern origin. For realism as expressed in literature is but the sentiment of the obvious and the true; and in the days when art was a splendid novelty, the first poets, as also the first painters, sought their inspirations directly from the primal source of all reality,—that is, from Nature herself.

Nature, therefore, is the mother of realism, artistically considered, and Homer was its first exponent; for not only was the actuality of his subject never neglected for the purely ideal, but it was also a first experience.

But the impressions produced by the real undergo in the mere transcription certain modifications, which are greater or less according to the organization of the exponent; and while some of the subject's delicate aroma invariably escapes in its passage, however transitory, from brain to canvas, the proper conservation of what remains constitutes the work of art on whose opulence succeeding generations are nourished, and from which, in turn, other impressions are derived; and where the original exponent has artistically transcribed that which he has seen and felt, his followers express not that which reality suggests to them, but that which Nature suggested to him, and the original types of the one become the modified models of the others, until in descending the centuries reality becomes unrecognizable, and art and literature through constant copying of copies become at last enervated and meaningless.

When, therefore, the poetry of the Greeks was becoming entangled in the subtleties of versification, it received a fresh and vigorous impulsion from Theocritus, who, disregarding the set rules of his contemporaries, and returning to the direct observation of reality, expressed not only the ideal, as poetry should, but also Nature in her most humble and familiar details, and represented his Shepherdess as beautiful but unkempt, the odor of cattle about her, and with her hands hardened by contact with the horns of the steers. Pictures of the obvious and the true should represent, therefore, not only the beautiful but the repulsive, not only that which is unpleasant but that which is agreeable; and the Shepherdess of Theocritus, in her unkempt beauty, would be as untrue to nature had she not the odor of the cattle about her as are the patched and powdered bergères with which Watteau charmed the Pompadour.

Nature loves and abounds in contrasts, as witness the toad squatting beneath the rose bush; and while either may afford a separate study, yet the union of the two is necessary in a faithful picture of what actually exists.

When, therefore, Villon broke away from the stilted and flowery madrigals of the school of Charles d'Orléans, and sought anew for the simplicity of Nature, he was but continuing Theocritus and paving the way for Diderot and Rétif de la Bretonne. The current of opinion, however, was adverse to these writers, and it was not until the early part of the present century, when the Romantic school, with its vanguards led by Madame de Staël and Chateaubriand and with Victor Hugo for its subsequent chief, had succeeded after a terrible struggle in freeing themselves from the established rules and conventional phrasing of the classicists and had raised the standard of liberty in art, that many of the prejudices which the Academicians had engendered disappeared, and the ground, swept clean and clear, was prepared for the advent of a new teacher.

It was at this propitious moment that Balzac, already famous through his "Physiologie du Mariage," presented his credentials in the "Peau de Chagrin," and with an audacity unparalleled in literature represented his hero as troubled not only about the state of his mistress' affections, but also as to whether he would have money enough to pay her fare in a cab.

The stupefaction and indignation of the purists at this unheard-of infraction of their formal style were indescribable, but the Romantic school upheld the innovation, and the new generation applauded the realistic portrayal of the penniless student who went to an evening entertainment on the points of his shoes, while dreading a splash of mud more than a shot from a pistol.

In this respect, therefore, the "Peau de Chagrin" marked the first return in the nineteenth century to the real and to the true; it gave a fresh impulse to an expiring literature, and constituted the corner-stone of the Realistic school, which has found such able exponents not only in the De Goncourts and Flaubert, but in Dickens, Thackeray, Tourgénieff, and a host of lesser lights.

But Balzac's incontestable superiority over other writers consists in his descriptions of the habits and customs of every-day life, and in his perception and rendition of the delicate and innumerable shadings which accompany their thousand complications, in the scenes of private life which he depicted, in the little mysterious dramas which take place every day in every social sphere, and especially in his portraits. The exactitude of the transcription, the delicacy of the shading, and the profusion and realism of detail are such that it would almost seem as though reality itself had been transported and placed before the eyes of the reader.

The third and last number of the "Revue Parisienne" contains a criticism of Balzac's on the "Chartreuse de Parme," in which, in alluding to the author, he says, "Stendhal is one of the most remarkable writers of the day, but in his work form is neglected; he writes as a bird sings."

Form, the absence of which he noticed in Stendhal, was to him a source of continued care and preoccupation, and he would often spend an hour in burnishing a single sentence. With all his facility of conception, execution was exceedingly laborious, and his admiration of Gautier's ability to dash off without an erasure a warm-colored and impeccable article, while unbounded, was not unmixed with a certain conviction that the work would be improved by a thorough revision.

As has been seen, Balzac spent almost ten years in forming his hand and chastening his style, and the courage which he then manifested was equaled only by the patience with which he sought to improve the coloring of his afterwork. As a grammarian he is unsurpassed, and the faults which are noticeable in many of his works are for the most part purely clerical, and due to his mania for writing his books on proof-sheets instead of in manuscript. As an innovator he was of course attacked,—all innovators are,—and Sainte-Beuve, whose manner of writing Balzac had characterized as macaroni, continually ridiculed his style and form of expression. In this respect, however, it should be remembered that at the time of Balzac's advent into literature the French language had been passed through a strainer so fine that no terms remained to express anything beyond the purely conventional; and Balzac, who was thoroughly impressed with Aristotle's idea that the inexpressible does not exist, was almost obliged to create a language of his own; and in his endeavor to express himself with realistic clearness he seized upon every suggestive technicality which he encountered in science, in the green room, the alcoves of the hospital, or the by-ways of Paris, and built a vocabulary from all that was most expressive in the different strata of existence. It was he who invented "chic" and many other terms of an equally felicitous nature.

"As for neologisms, as the critics call them," he said, "who, I would like to know, has a right to give alms to a language, unless it be its writers? Of course I create words, but my parvenus will become nobles in time."

But through discipline and constant attention Balzac's style assumed at last the undulatory rhythm of the Romantic school, and became not only picturesque, mathematical, and peculiarly incisive, but the model of many of the prominent writers of to-day.

The attacks of the critics were not confined, however, to his style and form of expression; charges of personal as well as literary immorality were brought against him, and it is curious to note that while Venice reveled through an entire carnival in a masquerade of his characters his books were prohibited in Rome and Madrid.

Personally considered, Balzac was much more of a Benedictine than a disciple of Rabelais; even his student days were those of an anchorite, and purity of life was to him not only a refinement, but a basis indispensable to elevation of thought, and an essential in the production of any work of enduring value. Disorder he regarded as fatal to talent, and Gautier says that he preached what he practiced, and recommended to him that he should visit his Dulcinea but once a year, and then only for half an hour. "Write to her, if you wish to," he said; "it forms the style." In his books he has, it is true, agreeably painted the seductions of vice, but its contagious and destructive effects are rigorously exposed; and through all the struggles of his characters probity, purity, and self-denial are alone triumphant. In what, then, does his immorality consist? In his vast conception, it was necessary, he explained,[17] here to signalize an abuse and here to point out an evil; but every writer who has an aim and who breaks a fresh lance in the domain of thought is invariably considered immoral. Socrates was immoral; Christ was immoral: both were persecuted by the people whom they reformed.

In describing in the "Comédie Humaine" all the elements of society, in grasping it in the immensity of its agitations, it was inevitable that one part should expose more wickedness than virtue, that one part of the fresco represented a culpable group: hence the critic has brought his charge of immorality without observing the morality of other parts destined to form a perfect contrast. And in this particular we must observe that the most conscientious moralists are agreed that society is incapable of producing as many good as evil actions, yet in the "Comédie Humaine" the virtuous characters exceed in number those of a reprehensible disposition.

Blamable actions, faults, crimes, from the slightest to the most grave, find therein an invariable punishment, human or divine, evident or secret; and while it would be impossible to clothe two or three thousand characters in white and

---

[17] Preface to the *Comédie Humaine.*

orange blossoms, it must be evident even to the most careless observer that the Marneffes, male and female, the Hulots, Brideaus *e tutti quanti*, are not imagined,—they are simply described.

CHAPTER III.

THE BUSKIN AND THE SOCK.

"Le génie, c'est la patience." —Buffon.

In the story of "Albert Savarus" Balzac drew a picture of the hero which, with slight modifications, might have served as his own.

He was tall and somewhat stout. His hands were those of a prelate, and his head was that of a Nero. His hair was black and dense, and his forehead, furrowed by sabre-cuts of thought, was high and massive. His complexion was of an olive hue; his nose was prominent and slightly arched; his mouth was sympathetic, and his chin firm. But his most remarkable characteristic was the expression of his gold-brown eyes, which, eloquent with interrogations and replies, seemed, instead of receiving light from without, to project jets of interior flame.

His many vicissitudes had endowed him with an air of such calm tranquillity as might have disconcerted a thunderbolt; while his voice, at once penetrating and soft, had the charm attributed to Talma's.

In conversation persuasive and magnetic, he held his auditors breathless in a torrent of words and gesture. He convinced almost at will, and his imagination, once unbridled, was sufficient to cause a vertigo. "He frightens me," said Gérard de Nerval; "he is enough to drive one crazy."

"He possessed," Gautier said, "a swing, an eloquence, and a *brio* which were perfectly irresistible. Gliding from one subject to another, he would pass from an anecdote to a philosophical reflection, from an observation to a description. As he spoke, his face flushed, his eyes became peculiarly luminous, his voice assumed different inflections, while at times he would burst out laughing, amused by the comic apparitions which he saw before describing, and announced, in this way, by a sort of *fanfare*, the entrance of his caricatures and witticisms. The misfortunes of a precarious existence, the annoyances of debt, fatigue, excessive work, even illness, were unable to change this striking characteristic of continual and Rabelaisian joviality."

Friends, enemies, editors, strangers, money-lenders, and usurers, all with whom he came in contact, were fascinated and coerced by the extraordinary magnetism which he exerted without effort, and the most vigorous intellects were bewildered by his projects of fortune and dreams of glory.

Attracted by the mine of wealth which the theatre opens to the popular playwright; and burdened with a real or imaginary weight of debt, from which one or two dramas, if favorably received, would free him entirely; and desirous, moreover, of experiencing the delirious intoxication which the plaudits of the gallery bring to the successful dramatist, Balzac's inflammable imagination became a veritable whirlwind of plots and epigrams whenever a new play was well received.

But for the playwright, as for the mechanic, an apprenticeship is obligatory, and, though Balzac's novels contained action and analysis, drama and observation, it was not, as we have seen, until after a long and laborious preparation that he was enabled to attract the attention of the public; and it is evident that the heights which he then scaled were so fatiguing and time-consuming that his life, wearied by the struggle, was not of sufficient duration to permit his winning equal triumphs on the stage.

From his early schooldays, however, in which, it will be remembered, he commenced a tragedy on the Incas, which was afterwards followed by a drama in blank verse entitled "Cromwell," the stage had possessed an irresistible attraction for him; and if therein he was not at first successful, it was perhaps from the very cause which brought to him his original popularity, and the superabundance of his ideas, paradoxical as it at first appears, was undoubtedly his greatest stumbling-block.

To imagine a plot was nothing, the scenes were but details, and the outline of a melodrama was to him the work of as little labor as would be required in the conception of a pleasing menu; but when the general plan was sketched, each scene would suggest a dozen others, and the Coliseum of Vespasian would not have been large enough to present the simultaneous action which the play, at once interminable and impossible, would have demanded.

Another reason for his lack of immediate success was the jealousy of his colleagues and the hatred of the critics; and as at that time the existence of a play depended entirely upon the manner in which the first representation was received, it was not very difficult to create a cabal against this usurper, who, not content with his legitimate celebrity, seemed, at the bare mention of a play, to meditate a universal literary monarchy, in which he would reign supreme; and while the conquest of both spheres has been effected by Hugo, Voltaire, and others of like ilk, yet these authors were careful to fortify their progress with a book in one hand and a play in the other, whereas it was not until Balzac had reached his apogee that he began a serious attack on the stage.

It was in the year 1840 that Balzac submitted "Vautrin," his first drama, to the director of the Porte-St.-Martin. The play was at once accepted; for the author's reputation was not only gigantic, but the Porte-St.-Martin had almost foundered in successive tempests, and to the director, who was as penniless as he was appreciative, the offer was little less than a godsend. An agreement was signed forthwith, and Balzac abandoned Les Jardies for more convenient quarters, where he could attend to the rehearsals and remodel the scenes on the stage itself, which, it may be added, he continued to do up to the very last moment.

During these preparations, the boulevards were agog with excitement. The actors and the director, accompanied by Balzac's friends, wandered daily from the Boulevard Bonne Nouvelle to Tontoni's and the Café Riche, exciting the curiosity of the *flaneurs* by their reticence or murmured confidences; and Balzac's ingress and egress from the theatre were, it is said, watched and waited for by curious crowds.

Never in the history of the drama had a first representation been so impatiently awaited; and Balzac, foreseeing the immense sale which the seats would have, bought up the entire house, and then, while endeavoring that the tickets should circulate only among his friends and their acquaintances, sold the better part of it over again at a large advance.

"My dear friend," he wrote to Dablin, "if among your acquaintances there are any who wish to assist at the first representation of 'Vautrin,' let me know who they are, as I prefer to let the boxes to those whom I know about, rather than to those who are unknown to me. I particularly wish to have handsome women present. The demand for boxes is greater than the supply. The journalists are to be sacrificed."

To Gozlan he wrote,—

"I have sent you a ticket for the stalls. The rehearsals have almost killed me. You will witness a memorable failure. I have been wrong, I think, to summon the public.

"Morituri te salutant, Cæsar!"

Unfortunately, the interval between the sale of the seats and the first representation was sufficiently great to permit of two thirds of the tickets falling into the hands of those who were unknown or hostile to Balzac; and consequently, when the great day arrived, the critics sharpened their knives, and in place of the indulgent friends and handsome women whom Balzac had expected to welcome his play the theatre was crowded with malevolent faces.

The title-rôle was taken by Frédéric Lemaître, and while the first three acts were received without any demonstrations, either of approval or disapprobation, over the fourth there burst a tempest which, since the birth-night of "Hernani," was unequaled in the annals of the stage; for Lemaître, reappearing in the costume of a Mexican general, seemed—whether by accident or design, it has never been clearly understood—to present an insulting resemblance to Louis Philippe, whose eldest son happened to be in one of the most conspicuous boxes.

The entire house, from pit to gallery, re-echoed with hisses and catcalls. Threats and even blows were exchanged, for here and there, in spite of the general indignation, a few still remained faithful to Balzac.

Through Lemaître's eccentricity, the battle was lost and the drama killed. Further representations were prohibited by the government; and though, a few days later, M. de Rémusat called upon Balzac, and offered in the name of the state an indemnity for the pecuniary loss which he had sustained, it was haughtily refused. "If my play was justly prohibited, there is," he said, "no reason why I should be indemnified; if it be otherwise, I can accept nothing, unless an indemnity be also made to the manager and actors of the Porte-St.-Martin."

Two years after the failure of "Vautrin," and entirely unaffected by its sudden collapse, Balzac knocked at the door of the Odéon which was at that time under the management of Lireux. By this gentleman Balzac was received with the greatest cordiality; for while his first play had fallen flat, yet it had fallen with such a crash that, in the lapse of time, it was difficult to distinguish its failure from success. Moreover, the Odéon was bankrupt, and as Balzac, with his customary enthusiasm, offered nothing less than a Golconda in his manuscript, he was fêted, caressed, and altogether received with open arms.

From the office to the green room, from the door-keeper to the scene-shifters, smiles, compliments, and welcomes were showered upon him, and he was unanimously requested to read his play at once. As soon, therefore, as the actors were assembled and silence obtained, Balzac began to read "Les Ressources de Quinola." At first thick and embarrassed, his voice gradually grew clearer, and expressed the most fugitive undulations of the dialogue. His audience laughed and wept by turns, and Balzac laughed and wept with them; the entire troop was fascinated, and applauded as only actors can. Suddenly, however, at the end of the fourth act, Balzac stopped short, and explained in the simplest and most unaffected manner that, as he had not yet written the fifth, he would be obliged to recite it to them.

The stupor and surprise of his audience can be more readily imagined than described: for the fifth act of "Quinola" is the unraveling of all the tangled threads, the union of all the joints; it is the climax and logical termination of all that has gone before; and Balzac, as he calmly rolled up his manuscript and tied it with a bit of string, easily, fluently, and unhesitatingly continued the drama through the six final scenes, and without a break, without a pause, through a torrent of varied intonations, led his listeners by a magnificent tour de force to the very fall of the curtain.

Lireux was bewildered and entranced. "The rehearsals shall commence to-morrow," he said. "But to what address, M. de Balzac, shall I send the announcements?"

"It is unnecessary to send any," Balzac replied. "I can come without them."

"Ah, no, that is impossible. There will be a rehearsal one day, and none the next; and I never know until the morning at what hour a rehearsal is to take place. What is your address?"

But Balzac had not the least intention of telling where he lived, and either because he was playing hide-and-go-seek with his creditors, or else was at that time possessed of one of the inexplicable manias which caused him at times to keep his habitat a secret even from his most intimate friends, he refused flatly to impart the wished-for information.

"I do not see what we can do," Lireux murmured helplessly, "unless we use a carrier pigeon."

"I do," replied Balzac, ever fertile in expedients. "Listen to me. Send a messenger up the Champs-Élysées with the notice every morning at nine o'clock. When he reaches the Arc de l'Étoile, let him turn to the left, and he will see a man beneath the twentieth tree, who will pretend to be looking up in the branches for a sparrow."

"A sparrow?"

"A sparrow or any other bird."

"My pigeon, perhaps."

"Let me continue. Your messenger will approach my sentinel, and will say to him, 'I have it.' Thereupon my sentinel will reply, 'Since you have it, what are you waiting for?' Then your messenger will hand the notice to him, and immediately go away, without once looking behind him. I will attend to the rest."

Lireux saw no objection to this fantastic whim, and contented himself by expressing the hope that if the twentieth tree should be destroyed by lightning M. de Balzac would see no insuperable objection to posting his sentinel at the twenty-first.

"No," Balzac answered, "but I should prefer the nineteenth; the number is more quaint."

This plan amicably arranged, the actors agreed upon, and the date of the first representation settled, Balzac proceeded to talk finance.

"Beside the customary royalty, I wish the entire house for the first three nights."

"But what shall I get?" Lireux timidly inquired.

"Half the profits, which will be incalculable."

Lireux reflected for a moment. "Very good," he said; "I accept."

From the first rehearsal Balzac recommenced with "Quinola" the treatment to which "Vautrin" had been subjected. Sometimes a phrase was altered, sometimes a scene, while at others an entire act was remodeled. That which pleased him one day displeased him the next, and each rehearsal brought fresh corrections and alterations, until the original manuscript was entirely obliterated with erasures and new ideas.

Besides undergoing the mental and physical labor attendant on these rehearsals, Balzac undertook the entire charge of the sale of the seats, or rather the entire charge of refusing seats to all comers; for the box office was opened merely for form's sake, and tickets were to be had only of Balzac in person. To obtain one was not so much a question of money as of position and influence. The orchestra stalls he reserved for the nobility, the avant-scènes for the court circle; the boxes in the first gallery were for the ambassadors and plenipotentiaries; the second gallery was for the statesmen, the third for the moneyed aristocracy, the fourth for the select bourgeoisie. "As for the critics," he said, "they can buy their seats, if there are any left, and there will be none."

As a rule, therefore, when any one asked for a box, Balzac would reply, "Too late: last one just sold to the Princesse de Machin and the Grande Duchesse de

Chose." During the first few days of the sale, seats were in consequence sold at extraordinary prices; but later on the anxiety to obtain them decreased, and during the week preceding the first performance Balzac was very glad to dispose of them to any one at the regular rates.

On the 6th of March, 1842, thirteen days before the play was to be performed, he wrote to a friend as follows:—

"DEAR SOFKA,—Send me the address of the Princess Constantine Razumovska, that I may learn from her whether she wishes a box. Let me know also whether the two Princesses Troubetskoï want boxes, whether Kraïeska wishes one, whether the Malakoffs, and the Countess Léon, and the Countess Nariskine,—seven boxes in all. I must know, too, whether they want them in the upper or lower tier of the first gallery. I wish the handsome women in front.... It is a favor to be admitted to this solemnity. There are at the theatre a hundred and fifty applications for boxes from people whom I do not know and who will get nothing."

On the 12th he wrote to the same person: "The avant-scènes are for the king and the cabinet; they take them by the year. I can only give, therefore, to the Princess Troubetskoï a box in the first gallery, but it is one of the best in the house.... The costumes have cost 20,000 francs; the scenery is entirely new. Every one insists that the play is a masterpiece, and that makes me shudder. In any event, it will be a terrible solemnity. Lamartine has asked for a box; I will place him among the Russians. Every morning I receive thirty or forty applications, but I will have no one whom I do not know about.... Tell your Russian friends that I must have the names and addresses, *each accompanied by a written and personal recommendation* of those of their friends (men) who wish stalls. There are over fifty people a day who come under assumed names and refuse to give their address; *they are enemies, who wish to ruin the piece.* In a week I shall not know what I am about. We are obliged to observe the most severe precautions. I am intoxicated with the play."

The severe precautions resulted on the night of the first representation in a half-empty house.

Few imagined that seats could really be had, and it was even reported that Balzac had been obliged to refuse a seat to the Duc de Nemours. The amateurs resigned themselves, therefore, almost without a struggle, and determined that as they could not obtain seats for the first performance they would find solace in the second or third; but on reading the articles which appeared the next day they felt little need of consolation, for the fate of "Vautrin" had been repeated, and "Quinola" had fallen flat. The most sympathetic of all the criticisms which then appeared was one contained in Le National for the 16th of March, 1842. It runs as follows:—

"The subject of M. de Balzac's drama was excellent, but unfortunately, through eccentricity or negligence, he passed but to one side of the idea, without resolutely entering it and extracting all its wealth.

"The Odéon is the theatre of tumultuous representations, but never has this terrible battle-field offered such a conglomeration of exclamations and confusing cries. The pit, like a sharp-shooter, took up an ambush behind the substantives and verbs, and slaughtered the play while it maimed the actors, who, brave though wounded, struggled on to the end with a praiseworthy and melancholy courage. At times the comedy, through its sudden flashes of originality and abrupt cannonades of wit, seemed about to rout the enemy and wave aloft a tattered but victorious flag. The faults, however, were too numerous and the errors too grave, and in spite of many advantages the battle, in the end, was fairly lost."

But in spite of the derision, insults, and abuse with which the first representation was received, in spite of the financial and dramatic shipwreck, after the commotion had subsided and the audience had dispersed, Balzac, superior to destiny and indifferent to fate, was found fast asleep and snoring in his box.[18]

In addition to "Vautrin" and "Quinola," three other plays of Balzac's have been produced, namely, "Paméla Giraud," "La Marâtre," and "Le Faiseur" ("Mercadet"), of which the first was performed at the Gaieté in September, 1843, and enjoyed a moderate success. Concerning the second, M. Hostein, formerly director of the Théatre-Historique, has offered some curious information.[19] Balzac, it appears, called upon him one day, and explained that for some time past he had been thinking over an historical drama for the Théatre-Historique.

"I shall call it," he said, "'Pierre et Catharine,' Peter the Great and Catharine of Russia. That, I think, would be an excellent subject."

"Treated by you, it could not be otherwise. But are you far advanced, M. de Balzac?"

"It is all here," Balzac answered, tapping his forehead. "I have but to write it out, and, if you care to, the first tableau can be rehearsed the day after to-morrow."

"Can you give me an idea of this first tableau?" I asked.

"Certainly. We are in a Russian inn. You can see it from here. In this inn plenty of action: the troops are passing by; soldiers come in, drink, chat for a moment, and then off again, but everything is done rapidly. Among the people of the inn is a servant-girl, young, active, and alert,—pay attention to her: her figure is good; she is not handsome, but she is peculiarly attractive. The soldiers jest with her; she smiles at every one, but her admirers are obliged to be careful, for any familiarity is answered with a slap, which is as good as a blow.

"A soldier enters who is more daring than the others. He is charged with a particular mission; his time, therefore, is his own. He can drink at his ease and chat with the servant, if she pleases him; for that matter, she pleases him at first sight, and she likes the soldier, too. 'Here,' he says, catching hold of her arm, 'sit down at this table and drink with me.'

"The soldier takes a seat, and the girl does the same. Noticing, however, some objection on the part of the innkeeper, he rises angrily, and strikes the table with his fist. 'If any one interferes with what I do, I will burn the whole shanty down.'

"And he would have done it, too. He is a good soldier, but terrible with his inferiors. The old innkeeper motions to the girl to obey. The soldier sits down again. He places one arm tenderly about the girl's neck, and then, having drunk deeply,

[18] *Balzac Chez Lui.* Léon Gozlan.
[19] *Le Figaro,* 20 October, 1876.

he whispers, 'I will give you a better home than this.' While they are talking together, inattentive to the others, the door at the back opens. An officer enters, and every one rises, with respect. The soldiers make the regulation salute, and stand motionless. The soldier and the servant alone remain seated. The officer notices this, and grows angry. He looks at the girl and advances toward the table; having reached the soldier, he raises his arm, and lets it fall with a terrible force on the shoulder of the poor devil, who bends beneath the shock.

"'Up, rascal!' the officer cries. 'Go write your name and regiment, and bring the paper to me.'

"At the first moment, that is to say on receiving the blow, without knowing by whom it had been directed, the soldier turns to avenge himself; but on recognizing his superior he rises automatically, salutes the officer, and goes to another table to obey the command. The officer, on his part, examines the servant with renewed attention. Her appearance pleases and calms him. The soldier returns, and respectfully presents his paper.

"'Very good,' the officer says, as he returns it to him. 'Off with you.'

"The soldier salutes him again, turns right about face, and marches off, without even looking at the girl. The officer, however, smiles at her, and she smiles at him.

"'A good-looking man,' she thinks.

"The good-looking man takes the seat previously occupied by the soldier, orders the best that the inn affords, and invites the servant to keep him company. She accepts without hesitation. The conversation begins, and they are soon quite friendly. A stranger appears at the doorway. He is enveloped in a long cloak. At his entrance, men and women fall on their knees; some of them even bend their foreheads to the ground. As was the case with the soldier, the officer does not notice what is going on behind him. His seductive companion has captivated him completely. In a moment of enthusiasm, the officer exclaims, 'You are divine! I will take you with me. You shall have a beautiful apartment, where it will be always warm.'

"From afar the stranger scrutinizes the couple, and, in spite of himself, the girl's sympathetic appearance attracts his attention. He approaches the table, and, throwing open his cloak, stands with his arms crossed on his breast.

"The officer looks around, and, immediately rising, bends on one knee, and stammers these words:—

"'Your pardon, sire!'

"'Rise.'

"Like the soldier, the officer then stands erect, awaiting the good pleasure of his master. The master, meanwhile, is engaged in looking at the servant, and she, in turn, is fearlessly admiring the all-powerful Czar.

"'You may go,' he says to the officer. 'I will keep this woman. She shall have a palace.'

"It was in this way that Peter the Great met for the first time the woman who afterwards became Catharine of Russia...

"And now tell me, what do you think of my prologue?"

"Very curious, very original; but the rest of it?"

"That you shall have in a little while; in the mean time, I am planning an entirely novel mise-en-scène. Russia is for our theatres, and especially for yours, an unexplored and fecund mine. We will be the first to introduce it."

Balzac left me in a state of great enthusiasm, and I built mountains of hopes on the inevitable success of "Pierre et Catharine."

When I saw him again, however, everything had changed. He had given up the Russian drama for the moment, but promised to complete it later on. He had, he said, thought it over. It was a colossal undertaking, in which nothing should be neglected; and as the details concerning certain ceremonies were wanting, he proposed to take a trip to Moscow during the winter, and study the subject on the ground itself. He begged me, therefore, not to insist upon its immediate production, and offered another play in the place of the one thus postponed.

In spite of my disappointment, I could, of course, do nothing but submit, and in sheer despair I asked him to tell me something of his new piece.

"It will be horrible," Balzac contentedly replied.

"How, horrible?"

"Understand me: it is not a question of a heavy melodrama, in which the villain burns the house down, and runs the inmates through and through,—not at all. My play is to be a simple comedy, in which everything is calm, tranquil, and pleasing. The men play placidly at whist, the women laugh and chat over their worsted work, everything announces harmony and order; but beneath this calm surface passions are at work, and the drama ferments, till at last it bursts forth like the flame of a conflagration."

"You are in your element, sir. Then your plot is found?"

"Completely. It was chance, our habitual collaborateur, that furnished me with it. I know a family,—whom I will not name,—composed of a husband, a daughter by a first marriage, and a stepmother, still young and childless. The two women adore each other. The little attentions of the one and the caressing tenderness of the other are admired by all who know them. I, too, thought it charming, at first; then I became surprised, not that a stepdaughter and stepmother should love each other,—for there is nothing unnatural in such an affection,—but that they should love each other so dearly. Excess spoils all things. I began, therefore, to observe them more closely, and a few trivial incidents served to confirm my impression that all was not as it appeared. Finally, a few evenings ago, all doubt on the subject was removed. When I entered the drawing-room, it was almost deserted, and I saw the daughter leaving the room without having seen me; in so doing, she glanced at her stepmother, and what a look she gave her! It was like the thrust of a dagger. The stepmother was engaged in putting out the candles on the whist-table. She turned to the girl; their eyes met, and the most gracious of smiles played on their lips. The door closed on the girl, and the expression on the stepmother's face changed suddenly to one of bitter contraction. All this, you will readily understand, passed like a flash of lightning; but I had seen quite enough, and I said to myself, Here are two creatures who loathe each other. What had happened? I do not know, and I never want to; but from that moment the entire drama unrolled before me."

"And for the first representation, you will, of course, offer a box to these ladies, that they may profit by the moral which your play will necessarily point?"

"Assuredly I shall do so; and since you mention it, I will be obliged if you will reserve an extra box for me. I have not, however, the slightest intention of teaching them a lesson, and I consider that a novelist or dramatist would be highly presumptuous did he write with such an object. An author should influence only through instinct or chance. To return, however, to these ladies: that they play a comedy of tenderness is to me beyond a doubt, but as between ourselves matters will, in all probability, rest where they are. My ferocious deductions are but the fruit of my imagination, and will never, I trust, have anything in common with the realities of their existence; but in the event of their disunion containing the germs of a violent climax, it is very possible that my play will pull them up with a round turn."

The months rolled on. Balzac went to Russia, and as soon as I heard of his return I called upon him at his residence in the Rue Fortunée. A servant in a red vest took my card, and a few moments later I was ushered into a low-ceilinged room. Balzac was at the other end of it, and cried out from afar, "Here is your manuscript!" Then I saw my author standing by his work-table, clothed in a long, monkish robe of white linen, with one hand resting on a mass of paper. I ran to him.

On the first page Balzac had written in large characters, "Gertrude, tragédie bourgeoise en cinq actes, en prose." On the back was the proposed distribution of the play. Melingue was designated for the rôle of Ferdinand, the lover of the stepmother and daughter; Madame Dorval was to play Gertrude; and the other parts were to be filled by Mathis, Barré, etc.

Beneath these names the author had minutely indicated everything which concerned the play,—the action, the furniture, and the decorations; he had even given the measure for the double carpet which he judged indispensable to the mise-en-scène.

It was then agreed that the play should be read the next day in the presence of Madame Dorval and Melingue. When, therefore, we had all assembled at the appointed time, he read it through from beginning to end, without stopping, and then quietly remarked, "It is much too long; it must be cut down a quarter." Not only did he cut it down, but he changed the title to that of "La Marâtre," which it has since so gloriously borne.

It was first represented in June, 1848, in the midst of the most disastrous political circumstances.... The theatres were necessarily abandoned, but such is the power of genius that all the bold and brave in literature who remained in Paris gathered that night, and received Balzac's work with the sympathy and applause which it so richly merited.

The next morning I paid him a visit. "We had quite a victory last night!" I joyously exclaimed.

"Yes," he answered; "a victory like that of Charles XII."

On taking leave of him, I asked where he had been during the representation. "Why," he answered, with a smile, "I was in a box with those ladies. They were greatly interested in the play. At the moment when Pauline poisons herself, that her stepmother may be accused of assassinating her, the young girl screamed with terror; the tears were in her eyes, and she looked reproachfully at me. Then she grasped her stepmother's hand, and raised it to her lips with a movement" —

"Of sincerity?"

"Ah, yes, indeed."

"You see, then, that your play may serve as a lesson."

Balzac's last play, "Le Faiseur," was produced for the first time at the Gymnase, a year after his death, under the title of "Mercadet." Its success was immediate, and its hundredth performance was the occasion of an article by Albéric Second in "Le Constitutionnel," 18 June, 1852, which is at once so graceful and fantastic that its reproduction here cannot fail to afford some pleasure to the readers of the "Comédie Humaine:" —

The hundredth performance of "Mercadet" was given the other evening at the Gymnase-Dramatique. "Mercadet" is, it will be remembered, the posthumous piece of M. de Balzac, which at the time of its production excited such great curiosity. Without any previous agreement, but none the less certain of meeting, a dozen of us, all passionate admirers of the illustrious deceased, found ourselves, that evening, intermingled with the line which from six o'clock in the evening had been undulating from the Boulevard Bonne Nouvelle to the door of the theatre. We had all assisted ten months before at the first representation of the play, and we piously reassembled at this jubilee of glory and genius in the same manner as we had gone the year before, and in the same manner that each year we shall go, on the 18th of August, to wreathe with immortelles the tomb of the great writer.

M. de Balzac was not one of those who inspire lukewarm affection, and they who have had the honor of knowing him preserve his memory religiously in their hearts. That life of his, full of struggles incessantly renewed, the hourly and truceless combat which he waged, sum up so completely the existence of the literary men of the nineteenth century that it is impossible for us to consider his grand and mournful figure otherwise than as the personification of an entire class. It is for this reason that God, who is sovereignly just, will accord to him hereafter a glory as great and incontestable as his life was tormented and sad. It is for this reason that it behooves us, who are the humble sacristans of the temple in which he was the radiant high priest, to see that his altars are ever adorned with fresh flowers and that the incense ceaselessly burns in the censers.

When we entered the theatre, it was, with the exception of a few boxes and a number of orchestra stalls which had been sold in advance, entirely filled. My seat was next to that of a gentleman apparently about forty-five years old. His bearing was exceedingly aristocratic; he was dressed with the most exquisite elegance, and his buttonhole bloomed with a rosette in which were intermingled in harmonious confusion all the orders of Europe and every shade of the rainbow. My neighbor was carelessly turning the pages of the "Entr'acte," and I took great pleasure in studying his well-poised head; wondering the while whether I had not met him somewhere before, and what his name might be. When he had finished reading he rose, turned his back to the stage, drew an opera-glass from his pocket, and began to examine the house; an E and an R, surmounted by a count's coronet, were engraved in letters of gold on the case which he placed on his seat. From time to time he bowed and waved his hand. My eyes mechanically followed the direction of his own, and I was not a little surprised at noticing that his smiles and salutations were addressed exclusively to the unoccupied boxes. When he passed all the boxes in review he turned his attention to the orchestra stalls, and the strange phenomenon was repeated. His opera-glass, flitting from stall to stall, stopped only at the empty ones; he would then bow, or make an almost imperceptible sign with the ends of his delicately gloved fingers. Dominated by that detestable pride which causes us to consider as insane all those whose actions or remarks are unintelligible to us, I murmured to myself, He is crazy. Then, as though he wished to remove the slightest doubt which I might have retained on this point, my neighbor bent over toward the seat at his left, and appeared to exchange a few words with an imaginary spectator. This seat was one of those which had been let in advance, and it was probable that its tenant, who was still absent, was interested only in the great play. I have omitted to state that the performance began with a little vaudeville.

At this moment one of my friends entered the orchestra, passed before me, shook my hand, and called me by name. My neighbor immediately turned around, gazed attentively at me for a moment or two, and then said,—

"Why, my dear fellow countryman,—for you are from La Charente, I believe,—I am delighted to see you."

"To whom have I the honor of speaking?" I asked, in great surprise.

My neighbor drew from his pocket a card, which he gallantly presented to me. My astonishment was so great that I almost screamed aloud; fortunately, however, I preserved my presence of mind. On the card, I read these words:—

"Le Comte Eugène de Rastignac."

"M. de Rastignac?" I repeated, incredulously.

"In person."

"The one who was born at Ruffec?"

"Precisely."

"The cousin of Madame de Beauséant?"

"Himself."

"Is it you who lived at the boarding-house kept by Madame Vauquer, née De Conflans?"

"Exactly."

"And who knew the Père Goriot and Vautrin?"

"Yes, indeed."

"You exist, then?" I stupidly inquired.

M. de Rastignac began to smile.

"Do you think that I present the appearance of a phantom?" he asked, as he gracefully twirled his moustache.

"Sir," I said, "I can readily understand that M. de Balzac should have borrowed your personality and extracted a great deal therefrom for the edification of his readers; but that he should have taken your name!—that, indeed, is something that I cannot believe."

"I had authorized him so to do."

"You?"

"Not only I did so, but all my friends did the same."

"All, you say?"

"Certainly."

"Of whom do you speak?"

"Of those who are in the theatre and to whom I have just bowed."

"But where are they?"

"Ah, yes; I forgot you cannot see them."

M. de Rastignac lightly touched my forehead with the forefinger of his right hand, and, light as was his touch, I immediately felt a violent electric shock, and it seemed as though I had undergone an operation similar to that of removing a cataract.

"Now look about you," said M. de Rastignac, and he pointed to the boxes and stalls which I had thought were empty. They were occupied by ladies and gentlemen, laughing and talking together in a most unghostlike fashion.

"They are almost all there," said Madame Vauquer's former lodger. "The principal personages of the 'Comédie Humaine' have, like you, come to salute the hundredth representation of 'Mercadet,' and their applause is so loud, *so loud*, that the echo of their bravos will rejoice Balzac in his tomb."

"Am I losing my reason?" I asked myself.

"I see that you are skeptical, my dear fellow," M. de Rastignac continued, "but let me give you a few proofs. Here is one which will satisfy you, I imagine;" and, turning about, he called to one of the spectators:—

"Nathan!"

"Well, my dear count?"

"Where and when is your next drama?"

"It will be given at the opening of the Ambigu-Comique."

"Will you send me a box?"

"Your name is already on the list."

"Du Bruel!"

"What is it?"

"You are becoming lazy, now that you are a member of the Académie."

"I? I have five acts in rehearsal at the Vaudeville and two at the Variétés."

"That is not so bad, then. But where is your wife?"

"Tullia? She is in the third box to the left."

"Alone?"

"With La Palférine."

"Bixion, your last caricatures were infamous."

"Bah! I would like to see you try your hand at them, with the censure at your heels."

"How are you, Lou de Lora? How are you, Stedman? Your exposition is superb. Ah, my friends, you are the princes of the Musée. But I say, Stedman, Pradier has just died: there is a fine place open."

"Yes; but then, alas, there are men who can never be replaced."

All these questions and answers bounded like the balls which two clever players serve and receive in a well-played game of tennis.

M. de Rastignac turned to me. "Are you as incredulous as before?" he smilingly inquired.

"I? God forbid, sir, that I should doubt your word."

In reality, however, I knew neither what to think nor what to believe, for I had curiously examined all these people whom my celebrated compatriot had addressed, and who, through M. de Balzac, as well as through their own achievements, were known and liked throughout civilized Europe. With the exception of Bixion, who was thin, poorly dressed, and not decorated, all the others appeared to be in the most flourishing state of health and fortune. Madame Tullia du Bruel was as appetizing as ever, and La Palférine, familiarly leaning on the back of her chair, exposed an ideal shirt and an impossible vest.

"Does M. de la Palférine no longer visit Madame de Rochegude?" I inquired.

"He is now entirely devoted to Tullia, and asserts that, after all, Du Bruel's cook is the finest artist in Paris."

"Is Madame de Rochegude still living?"

"She sits in that second box to the right."

"Who is with her?"

"Conti."

"The celebrated musician?"

"Yes, indeed. You remember the song,—

'Et l'on revient toujours,
A ses premiers amours.'"

It was with the greatest eagerness that I had turned to look at this artificial blonde, who had been so greatly beloved by the young Baron Calyste du Guénic. (Vide Béatrix.) A lace scarf was twisted about her neck in such a way as to diminish its length. She appeared worn and fatigued; but her figure was a masterpiece of composition, and she offered that compound of light and brilliant drapery, of gauze and crimped hair, of vivacity and calm, which is termed the je ne sais quoi.

Conti was also an object of great interest to me. He looked vexed, out of sorts, and bored, and seemed to be meditating on the eternal truth of that aphorism, profound and sombre as an abyss, which teaches that a cigar once out should never be relighted, and an affection once buried should never be exhumed.

"Is the Baron de Nucingen here?" I asked.

"Nucingen is confined to his bed with the gout; he has not two good months out of the twelve."

"And his wife?"

"The baroness no longer goes to the theatre. Religion, charity, and sermons occupy every instant of her time. Her father, Père Goriot, has now a white marble tomb and a perpetual resting-place in the cemetery of Père La Chaise."

"Where is her sister, Madame de Restaud?"

"She died a few years ago, legally separated from her husband."

"Pardon my insatiable curiosity," I said, "but ever since I was old enough to read and think I have not ceased to live with the personages of the 'Comédie Humaine.'"

"I am glad indeed," he courteously replied, "to be able to answer your questions. Is there anything that you still care to know?"

"What has become of the ex-minister of agriculture and commerce, the Comte Popinot, whom we called the little Anselme Popinot, in the days of the greatness and decadence of César Birotteau?"

"He followed the exiled princes to England."

"And Du Tillet?"

"Du Tillet is no longer in France."

"Did he leave for political reasons?"

"Is it possible that you did not hear of his failure! He absconded one day, with the till, ruined by Jenny Cadine and Suzanne du Val-Noble."

"Where are the children of Madame de Montsauf, that celestial creature, so justly called le Lys dans la Vallée?"

"Jacques died of consumption, leaving Madeleine sole mistress of an enormous fortune. In spite of what M. de Balzac said, I always supposed that she was secretly in love with Félix de Vandernesse. She is in that first avant-scène. She is an old maid now, but is none the less an adorable woman, and the true daughter of her mother."

"Do you know the name of that individual who has just entered her box?"

"That is Canalis."

"Canalis, the great poet, who played such an important part in the life of Modeste Mignon?"

"Precisely."

"I had thought that he was younger."

"He has grown quite old during these last few years. He has turned his attention to politics, and you may notice how politics hollows the cheeks and silvers the hair of poetry. He would bankrupt Golconda, however, and he is now attempting to win Mlle. de Montsauf and her millions. But look to the left, in that first box from the door of the gallery, and see whether you do not recognize one of the most curious physiognomies of the 'Comédie Humaine.'"

"Do you mean that stout woman?"

"Yes; it is Madame Nourrisau."

"Vautrin's aunt?"

"In flesh and blood, especially in flesh. There is the formidable hag who went one day to the son of the Baron Hulot and proposed, for fifty thousand francs, to rid him of Madame Marneffe. You must have read about it in 'La Cousine Bette.'"

"She is not alone, I see."

"She is with her husband."

"Her husband? Is it possible that she found one?"

"You forget that she is five or six times millionaire, and also the general rule that where it rains millions husbands sprout. Her name is now Madame Gaudessart, née Vautrin."

"Is it the illustrious Gaudessart who is the husband of that horrible creature?"

"Legally so, I beg you to believe."

"Speaking of the 'Cousine Bette,' can you tell me anything of Wencelas Steinbock and his wife?"

"They are perfectly happy. It is young Hulot who misbehaves; his wife is in that box over there, with the Steinbocks. Hulot has told them that he will join them later, and has probably stated that he had some urgent law business to attend to; but the truth is that he is behind the scenes at the opera. Hulot is not his father's son for nothing."

At this point M. de Rastignac smiled affectionately at a white-haired musician, who was tuning his violin.

"Is that the Cousin Pons?" I asked.

"You forget two things: first, that the Cousin Pons is dead; and secondly, that in his lifetime he always wore a green velvet coat. But though Orestes is no more, Pylades still lives. Damon has survived Pythias. It is Schmucke who sits before you. He is very poor; he has nothing but the fifty francs a month which he earns here, and the payment of a few piano lessons at seventy-five centimes each; but he will not accept any assistance, and, for my part, I have never seen tatters more proudly worn."

"Can you not," I asked, "show me M. Maxime de Trailles?"

"De Trailles no longer lives in Paris. When the devil grows stout he turns hermit. This retired condottiere is now a married man, the father of a family, and resides in the country. He makes speeches at the agricultural fairs, takes great interest in cattle, and represents his county at the general assembly of his department,—*the late* Maxime de Trailles, as he is now pleased to call himself."

"And Des Lupeaulx?"

"Des Lupeaulx is a prefect of the first class. But in place of these gentlemen, you have before you, in that box, the Count Félix de Vandernesse and the Countess Nathalie de Manerville; a little beyond, the Grandvilles and the Grandlieux; then, the Duke de Rhétoré, Laginski, D'Esgrignon Montreveau, Rochefide, and D'Ajuda-Ponto. Moreover, there are the Cheffrevilles; but then what a pity it is that our poor Camille Maupin is not present at this solemnity!"

"Is it of Mlle. des Touches that you speak?"

"Yes."

"Is she still religiously inclined?"

"She died like a saint, two years ago, in a convent near Nantes. She retired from the world, you remember, after accomplishing the marriage of Calyste du Guénic and Sabine de Grandlieu. What a woman she was! There are none like her now."

These last words of M. de Rastignac were covered by the three traditional knocks which precede the rise of the curtain.

"'Mercadet' is about to commence," he said.

"After the first act I will continue my gossip; provided, of course, that I do not weary you with it."

"Oh, my dear sir!" I cried. "My" —

I had not time to complete my phrase; a friendly but vigorous hand grasped my arm.

"So you come to 'Mercadet' to sleep, do you?" said a well-known voice.

"I? Am I asleep?"

"You are not asleep now, but you were."

I turned quickly around.

My neighbor was a fat-faced gentleman, with blue spectacles, who was peeling an orange with the most ridiculous gravity.

In the boxes and orchestra stalls, wherever I had thought to see the personages of the "Comédie Humaine," I found only insignificant faces, of the ordinary and graceless type, — a collection of obliterated medals.

At this moment the curtain rose, the actors appeared, and the great comedy of "Mercadet" was revealed, amid the applause and delight of the crowd.

I had been dreaming, therefore, and if I had been dreaming I must have been asleep. But what had provoked my somnolence? Was it the approach of a storm, the heat of the theatre, or the vaudeville with which the performance commenced?

Perhaps all three.

CHAPTER IV.

THE CHASE FOR GOLD.

"Nullum magnum ingenium sine mixtura dementiæ est." —
Seneca, De *Tranquillitate Animi*, c. 15.

From Balzac's early manhood his entire existence was consumed in a feverish pursuit of wealth; and had the mines of California been discovered at an earlier date, there is little doubt that he would have exchanged his pen for a pick, and sought, in a red shirt, to realize the millions with which he dowered his characters.

At the outset of his career, he was, as has been seen, unsuccessful in a business enterprise, and became, in consequence, heavily involved in debt. This spectre of the past haunted him so continually that it not only found frequent expression in his writings, in which money became a hymn, but it brought to him illusions and projects of fortune which were at once curious and fantastic.

At one time, shortly after the publication of "Facino Cane," —who, it will be remembered, was imprisoned in the dungeons of Venice, and, in making his escape, discovered the hidden treasures of the Doges, which he proposed to seek and share with his biographer, —Balzac became fairly intoxicated with the delusions of his hero, and his dreams of secreted wealth assumed such a semblance of reality that he at last imagined, or pretended that he had learned, the exact spot where Toussaint Louverture had buried his famous booty.

"'The Gold Bug' of Edgar Poe," Gautier writes, "did not equal in delicacy of induction and clearness of detail his feverish recital of the proposed expedition by which we were to become masters of a treasure far richer than Kidd's."

"Sandeau was as easily seduced as myself. It was necessary that Balzac should have two robust and devoted accomplices, and, in exchange for our assistance, he was good enough to offer to each of us a quarter of the prodigious fortune. Half was to be his, by right of conquest. It was arranged that we were to purchase spades and picks, place them secretly in a ship, and, to avoid suspicion, reach the designated spot by different roads, and then, after having disinterred the treasure, we were to embark with it on a brig freighted in advance. In short, it was a real romance, which would have been admirable had it been written instead of recited. It is of course unnecessary to add that the booty was not unearthed. We discovered that we had no money to pay our traveling expenses, and our united capital was insufficient to purchase even the spades."

At another time Balzac conceived the project of manufacturing paper from a substance which was at once cheap and plentiful. Experiments, however, proved that his plan was impracticable, and a friend who called to console him found that, instead of being dejected, he was even more jovial than ever.

"Never mind about the paper," he said. "I have a better scheme yet."

It was this: While reading Tacitus, he had stumbled upon a reference to the mines of Sardinia; his imagination, aided by his scientific knowledge, carried him back to the imperfect mechanical processes of old Rome, and he saw at once a vision of wealth, awaiting only modern appliances to be his own. With the greatest difficulty he collected—partly from his mother, partly from his cousin, and partly from that aunt whom the Anglo-Saxon Bohemian has converted into an uncle— the sum of five hundred francs; and then, having reached Genoa, he embarked for Alghiero, explaining his project to the captain of the vessel with the candor of an infant.

Once in Sardinia, dressed like a beggar,—a terror to brigands and monks,—he sought the mines on foot. They were easily found. With a few specimens of the ore, he returned immediately to Paris, where an analysis showed them to contain a large proportion of silver. Jubilant with success, he would then have applied to the Italian government for a concession of the mines, but unfortunately he was, for the moment, detained by lawsuits and other business, and when he at last set out for Milan it was too late. The perfidious captain had thought the idea so good that, without preliminary examinations, he had lost no time in securing an authorization in due form, and was then quietly proceeding to make a fortune.

"There is a million in the mines," Balzac wrote to his sister. "A Marseilles firm has assayed the scoriæ, but the delay has been fatal. The Genoese captain has already obtained a contract from the government. However, I have another idea, which is even better; this time there will be no Genoese. I am already consoled."

After having read "Venice Preserved" and admired the union of Pierre and Jaffier, Balzac says that he began to consider the peculiar virtues of those who are thrown outside of the social order,—the honesty of the galleys, the fidelity of robbers, and the privileges of that enormous power which these men obtain in fusing all ideas into one supreme will,—and concluded that, man being greater than men, society should belong entirely to those whose brilliancy, intelligence, and wealth could be joined in a fanaticism warm enough to melt their different forces into a single jet. An occult power of this description, he argued, would be the master of society; it would reverse obstacles, enchain desires, and give to one the superhuman power of all; it would be a world within a world, admitting none of its ideas, recognizing none of its laws; it would be a league of filibusters in yellow gloves and dogcarts, who could at all times be ready to devote themselves in their entirety to any one among them who should require their united aid.

This novel conception was not only the motif of the "Histoire des Treize," but no sooner was the book completed than Balzac, in accordance with his mania for living his characters, attempted to reproduce it in real life,—or rather, in the other life, for his true world was the one which he carried in his brain,—and without difficulty recruited for this purpose Jules Sandeau, Léon Gozlan, Laurent Jan, Gérard de Nerval, Merle, Alphonse Karr, and Granier de Cassagnac.

The aim of the association, which he explained with that tumultuous eloquence for which he was famous and which silenced every objection, was simply to grasp the leading-strings of the principal newspapers, invade the theatres, take seats in the Académie, and become millionaires and peers of France. When any one of them produced a book or a play, the others were to write about it, talk about it, and advertise it generally, until its success was assured; and as nothing succeeds like success, a good commencement was all that was needed to insure an easy and glorious ascent.

The project was enthusiastically received and unanimously approved. The society was entitled the "Cheval Rouge," and Balzac was elected chief.

In order to avoid suspicion, it was agreed that in public the members should not appear to know each other, and Karr relates that for a long time Balzac would pretend, whenever he saw him, that they met for the first time, and would communicate with him only in an actor's aside. The meetings of the society were pre-arranged by the chief. The notices consisted of a card, on which was painted a red horse, and the words, stable, such a day, such a place; in order to make it still more fantastic, the place was changed each time.

This project, which of course resulted in nothing, and which was soon abandoned, was none the less practicable, and minus the mysterious farce with which it was surrounded has since, in many instances, been put into successful operation.

Through one of those psychical phenomena which generate within us a diversity of sentiment while uniting their contradictory elements, Balzac was tortured by a combined distaste and affection for journalism. It possessed a morbid attraction for him; and while he execrated the entire profession, he longed none the less for an editor's chair, from which he could bombard his enemies at his ease, and glean at the same time the rich harvest which a successful review invariably produces.

The foundation of a journal, however, is money, more money, always money; and Balzac, who was rich only in unrecognized audacity and unquoted talent, after having tried in every way to acquire the necessary capital, was about to abandon his scheme as hopeless, when Providence in the form of a young man passed the sentries and entered his room.

"M. de Balzac?"

And Balzac, to whom every stranger was a dun, replied, "It is, sir, and it is not; it depends."

"I am looking for the author of 'La Peau de Chagrin.'"

"Ah! then, I am he."

"Sir," said the youth, "I understand that you are about to edit a journal, and I have come to ask for the position of theatrical critic. I would also like to write the fashion article."

Balzac, furious at the intrusion and indignant at the youth's proposition to collaborate in a journal whose appearance was prevented by lack of funds, was about to order the young man out, when he suddenly noticed that he was clothed in the most expensive manner.

"May I ask whom I have the honor of addressing?" inquired the ogre, with his most seductive smile.

"I am the son of M. Chose, the banker."

Balzac became very fascinating. "I thought so,—I thought so from the first; you look like him. Will you not sit down? As we were saying, I am about to edit the 'Chronique de Paris,' whose appearance, so impatiently awaited, I have delayed only that its success might be the better assured. And did I understand you to say that you would like to take charge of the theatrical criticisms?"

"Yes, indeed, sir, if you think me capable."

"Capable? Do I think you capable? Why, all the more capable, as it is unusual for a banker's son to wish to enter a purely literary association. The blood of a financier is seldom inclined to"...

"I do not care for letters of credit, M. de Balzac. I care for *letters*, simply."

"Adorable witticism!" cried Balzac, illuminated with hope. "And you care, then, for literature, in spite of the immense fortune which you enjoy?"

"I expect ten millions more," interrupted the youth.

"Ten millions!"

"Rather more than less, M. de Balzac."

"Nothing could be better or more opportune," smiled this courtesan of wealth, reduced to adulating an idiot. "I was just wondering whom I should select. The position is yours. No, no; it is for me to thank you. My best regards to your dear father."

The youth had barely turned the corner when Balzac hastily summoned the members of the "Cheval Rouge."

"At last I have a capitalist!" he cried. "He has promised nothing, it is true, but I have reason to believe that, properly managed, he will invest anywhere from a hundred thousand up. He is an idiot, the son of Chose the banker. He wants to be dramatic critic, and that means money, simply money, and lots of it. But," he continued, "the affair cannot be arranged without a subtle preparation and solemn initiation, and preparation and initiation mean *dinner*. It is at a dinner, not frugal but sumptuous, adorned with a garland of editors and critics, each more seductive than the other, that the alliance of your intelligence and the money of my imbecile will be consummated; and then, with the champagne in his throat, he will tell us how much he proposes to pour into the till of the 'Chronique de Paris.' It has not got one yet, to be sure, but we will buy one as soon as he furnishes the money."

"But there will be about twenty of us," objected de Nerval, "and the dinner will cost at least four hundred francs. Where are they? Have you got them?"

"No, but I will find them," Balzac answered, with a magnificent gesture. "It is not a question of a dinner in a restaurant, for that would smack of the adventurer a mile away; and besides, there of course you pay cash. The banquet shall be served here, and on credit. We have only to inspire some caterer with sufficient confidence."

"Charming," said Merle, as he looked about the poorly furnished apartment; "but how is that sufficiency of confidence to be inspired?"

After innumerable propositions had been discussed and rejected, Balzac discovered that Granier de Cassagnac had a service of silver in pawn for eight hundred francs, and prevailed on Gautier to borrow a like amount, disengage the silver, which, negligently exposed on Balzac's table, would inspire confidence in any caterer; promising that after the dinner the silver should be immediately repawned and the loan repaid.

"My plan is triumphant!" he exclaimed; "the money is ours. To-morrow we will liberate the silver. Tuesday, conference with the caterer. Wednesday, invitation on vellum launched at our young capitalist; the same evening, solemn engagement on his part to invest, accompanied on ours by the most hilarious toasts. Thursday, contract drawn by a notary and signed by the delicate hand of our millionaire. Friday, reunion and tea, to read over the prospectus, which I will compose. Saturday, colossal advertisement on every wall, monument, and column; and the week after, brilliant apparition on the Parisian horizon of the first number. Soldiers! to arms!"

This programme, joyously arranged, was fearlessly carried out. The silver was liberated, the caterer inspired with confidence, the invitation accepted, and after a sumptuous repast Balzac, glass in hand, arose and addressed the company as follows: —

"Gentlemen, you are all aware of the object for which we have assembled this evening about the liberal and gracious guest here seated at my right. It is the creation of a publication destined to assume, thanks to him and to his munificent intelligence, an unexceptionable position among the reviews of the century. Although I have not, to my great regret, been possessed of sufficient leisure to cultivate as I should have desired this rare intelligence, which has been called not only to fecundate our own, but also to assist us in spreading the fruits of our genius over a world which awaits them, and which, I may confidently state, would never know them save for the generous and effective assistance of our guest, I may nevertheless be permitted to say to what extent he has, in momentary confidences, permitted me to foresee treasuries of encouragement and rich rewards. I do not fear, therefore, to say that the 'Chronique de Paris' will owe to him its existence, its splendor, and its popularity. Were my emotion not so great and so real, I would speak at greater length of the future of our cherished and illustrious publication; but I prefer, in begging you, in honor of our guest, to join your toasts to mine, to leave the floor to him, that he may explain what in his generosity he proposes to do for the 'Chronique de Paris,' at once happy and proud to possess him as protector and patron."

Then, lowering his voice to one of simple politeness, Balzac turned to his guest, and said, "Be good enough, my dear young friend, to explain what your liberal intentions are."

"Gentlemen," the banker's son replied, "I will talk it over with papa."

Balzac grew white as the table-cloth, but, magnificent in his defeat, hardly had the pseudo-capitalist disappeared than he exclaimed, with an accent which might have unsettled destiny itself, "It is daylight; let us repawn the silver!"[20]

Partly for the sake of solitude, and partly to affect, for business purposes, an appearance of luxury, Balzac, in 1837, built a villa at Ville d'Avray, which he named Les Jardies, as a reminiscence of the days when Louis XIV. lounged at Versailles.

It consisted of but three rooms, or rather three stories. The ground floor, the *rez-de-chaussée*, was the reception-room, the second the study, and the third the bedroom.

When the architect's plan was first submitted, the staircase greatly interfered with the dimensions of the rooms, and Balzac, exasperated at this impertinence, ordered it out of the house, and caused it, by way of punishment, to climb in spiral solitude about the outer wall.

This little eccentricity gave to his parrot's cage the appearance of having been transplanted from some old Hanseatic or Flemish town, and satisfied at the same time his proprietary pride.

At a little distance was another habitation, in which the kitchen and servants' rooms were situated; and the whole establishment was surrounded by a high wall, which, being built on the incline of a hillock, was devastated by every storm, and fell five times into his neighbor's grounds; until Balzac, wearied by constant summons and complaints, bought the surrounding property, that his cherished wall might lie at ease where it chose.

The interior of Les Jardies was fully in keeping with the character of its owner. The reception-room was but scantily furnished, and the bare walls were ornamented with a promise of Gobelin tapestry traced in charcoal.

On the ceiling was written, "Fresco by Delacroix." On the wall of his study he wrote, "Here is a regal Venetian mirror," while a corner of his bedroom assured the visitor that he was looking at one of Raphael's priceless Madonnas.

In this way Balzac furnished his home with magnificent dreams, while he dined, perhaps, as did that creation of Dickens, who cut his bread into imaginary omelets, and sliced it into tenderloins.

Before Balzac's advent, the plot of ground on which Les Jardies was built had been a vineyard, on which the warm sun had lain all day, and ripened the clustering grapes. The knowledge of this fact preoccupied him greatly. If grapes had grown there, he argued, why should not anything else? Why should not pine-apples?

---

[20] *H. de Balzac*, by Eugène de Mirecourt. *H. de Balzac*, by Armand Bashet. *Balzac en Pantoufles*, by Léon Gozlan.

Now pine-apples were dear in Paris, costing from ten to fifteen francs apiece; and no sooner did this idea present itself than it was grappled, seized, and caressed by Balzac, who immediately saw an annual harvest of an hundred thousand pine-apples, which had bloomed in hot-houses as yet unbuilt.

These pine-apples would, he thought, sell at least for five francs apiece; the attendant expenses could not be over a hundred thousand francs; and by a simple mathematical process, with which no one was more familiar, he foresaw a princely revenue of four hundred thousand francs more.

These four hundred thousand francs danced with such charm and grace before him that he lost no time in looking for a shop in which to sell his unplanted fruit. He soon found a suitable one on the Boulevard Montmartre, which he would have immediately hired, painted in black and yellow, and decorated with an enormous sign, bearing for epigraph Pine-apples from Les Jardies, had he not been forcibly dissuaded by friends less enthusiastic than he.

In this way scheme succeeded scheme, and one project was abandoned only for another. His latest idea he always considered his best, unless he was agreed with, when he would reverse all his arguments to prove that a precedent one was better still. At one time he thought that through a mathematical combination he had discovered a system which would enable him to break the bank at Baden; at another he proposed to cut down a forest in Poland, and supply Paris with timber, and would have done so had not his brother-in-law proved to him that the expenses for transportation would far exceed any possible profit.

To make money, to become a millionaire, and to lead the life of a prince was his constant aim and ambition.

"The life of an artist," he said, "should be a succession of splendors;" and while he detested Dumas, he secretly admired his Oriental magnificence and envied his prodigal luxury. But while the firm of Dumas and Company was manufacturing novels by the dozen, Balzac was engaged in weighing a phrase and occupied with its corrections; while Dumas never so much as glanced at the proof-sheets of his feuilletons, Balzac's were not only carefully corrected, but the attendant expenses were, by agreement, charged to him; and where, as in the case of "Pierrette," he was obliged to pay for the corrections three hundred francs more than he received for the story itself, it will be readily understood that the amounts which he earned by his pen were not always as satisfactory as could have been desired.

In this respect, however, it should be stated that while the money which he earned in his later years was out of all proportion to that which he at first received, yet, in the mean time, some few debts had necessarily accumulated, and his income, consequently reduced, averaged at best not more than ten or twelve thousand francs.

The history of his financial troubles, and of that which he laughingly termed his floating debt, can best be found in his correspondence, which, ranging from his twentieth year to but a few days prior to his death, contains many details of the thirty years' war which he waged with poverty; and his letters, while interesting in their account of his transient successes, attendant struggles, defeats, and final victory, will convince even the prejudiced reader, that the writer was, in the first place, a man of the strictest integrity; for it may be said, without exaggeration, that the better part of his life was passed in attempting to satisfy that necessity whose earthly representatives are creditors; secondly, that his morals were perfectly pure, for he loved and reverenced women with that *amor intellectualis* which made chastity to him one of those graces which are superfluities to the vulgar and necessities to the re-fined; and thirdly, that his heart, which was as great as his brain, was yet too full of affection, for those whom he loved to harbor malice against his detractors and persecutors.

The earliest of these letters, the majority of which are addressed to his sister, or to Madame Zulma Carraud, one of her intimate friends, are mere descriptions of his life and poverty, and are expressed with the smiling indifference of youth, to whom the shadows of the future are yet vague and distant.

"Since you are so much interested in all that I do," he wrote from Paris to his sister, in 1819, "you must know that last night I slept magnificently; and how could I do otherwise? I dreamed of you, of mother, of my loves, of my hopes, and now, on awakening, I give you my earliest thoughts. I must tell you, in the first place, that that wretch, Myself, becomes more and more negligent. He goes but twice a week for provisions, and then, being economical even of his steps, always to the nearest, and consequently to the worst, shops in the neighborhood; hence, your brother, destined to such celebrity, is already nourished like any other great man, which means that he is dying of hunger."

To his sister, in the following year, he wrote,—

"I feel to-day that wealth does not constitute happiness, and that my life here will be to me always a source of the sweetest remembrances. To live as I choose; to work when I will, and after my own manner; to do nothing, even, if I so desire; to fall asleep in a beautiful future; to think of you, and to know that you are happy; to possess the Julie of Rousseau for mistress, La Fontaine and Molière for friends, Racine for master, and Père-Lachaise for promenade!... Oh, could it but last forever!"

And a little later,—

"I have just returned from Père-Lachaise, where I have been inhaling magnificent inspirations. Decidedly, the only beautiful epitaphs are such as these, *La Fontaine, Molière, Masséna,*—a single name which tells all, and makes the passer dream!"...

The next year he wrote,—

"Dear Sister,—I am going to work like the horse of Henri IV. before it was cast in bronze; and this year I hope to make the twenty thousand francs which are to commence my fortune. I have a quantity of novels and dramas to prepare.... In a little while there will be, between the me of to-day and the me of to-morrow, the difference that exists between the boy of twenty and the man of thirty. I reflect; my ideas ripen; and I see that in giving to me the heart and head which I possess Nature has treated me with favor. Believe in me, dear sister; for while I do not despair of being something, some day, I yet have need of a believer. I see now that

'Cromwell' had not even the merit of an embryo. As to my novels, they are as poor as the devil, though not half so seductive."

But when, later on, at the age of twenty-seven, Balzac found himself without position, without a profession, entirely unknown, without resources, and burdened, moreover, with a debt of 120,000 francs,—the result of his disastrous experience as printer and publisher,—he had but his pen with which to conquer poverty and combat the world. His family had no faith in him; they had sunk a large sum in his enterprise; he was friendless, and his genius was entirely unrecognized; and it is at once curious and pathetic to note through the rest of his correspondence the continued recurrence and repetition of his dream of prospective fortune and freedom from debt.

His first letters after his disaster are profoundly sad: in one he wrote to his sister,—

"I must live without asking aid of any one. I must live to work, that I may repay you all; but shall I be able to live long enough to pay my debts of love and gratitude as well?"

To the Duchesse d'Abrantès, in the same year, he wrote,—

"I wonder if you have ever experienced the extent to which misfortunes develop within us the terrible faculty of breasting a tempest, and of opposing to adversity an immobile calm.

"As for myself, I have acquired the habit of smiling at the torments of fate,— torments that still continue.

"I am old in suffering, but my light-hearted appearance offers no criterion of my age. I have never been otherwise; I have been always bent beneath a terrible weight. Nothing can give you an idea of the life which I have led, nor of my astonishment at having nothing but fortune to combat.

"Were you to inquire about me, you would be unable to obtain any insight to the nature of my misfortunes; but then you know there are those who die without any apparent disease....

"I have undertaken two books at a time, to say nothing of a number of articles. The days evaporate in my hands like ice in the sunlight. I do not live; I waste away; but death from work or from any other cause amounts to the same thing in the end.... I sleep from six in the evening until midnight, and then I work for sixteen hours. I have but one hour of liberty, and that during dinner. I have sworn to owe nothing, and though I die like a dog my courage will support me to the end."

In 1831, he wrote to the same lady,—

"You do not know that in 1828 I had but my pen with which to live and pay off 120,000 francs. In a few months I shall be free from debt, and be able to arrange a comfortable home. During the next six months, therefore, I shall enjoy my last miseries. I have asked aid from no one. I have never stretched my hand, either for a page or a sou. I have hidden my griefs and my wounds, and you who know how difficult it is to make money with the pen will, with your feminine glance, be able to sound the depths of the abyss which I disclose to you, and by the side of which I have marched without falling."

In the following year, he wrote to his mother,—

"Sooner or later, literature, politics, journalism, marriage, or some good speculation will make my fortune."

And later on,—

"Thank you, my sister; you have restored to me that energy which has been my sole support. Yes, you are right. I will not stop; I will continue to advance, and some day you will see mine counted among the great names of our country.... My books are the only replies which I shall make to those who commence to attack me. Do not let their criticisms annoy you: they are the best of auguries; mediocrity is never discussed. Tell my mother that I love her as I did when a child. The tears fall from my eyes as I write these lines,—tears of tenderness and of despair, for I feel my future near at hand, and in my days of triumph my mother will be a necessity. When will they come? As to you and to your husband, I can only hope that you will never doubt my heart, and if I do not write to you let your tenderness be indulgent. Do not misjudge my silence, but say, rather, 'He thinks of us, he is speaking to us;' for, after my long meditations and overwhelming duties, I rest in your hearts as in some delicious spot where there is no pain."

In the same year, from Aix, he wrote to his mother,—

"I shall not return to Paris until all my engagements are fulfilled; when I do so everything will have been paid off."

In 1833, to Madame Carraud,—

"My life is mechanically changed. I go to sleep with the chickens and am called at one in the morning. I then work until eight o'clock, sleep for an hour, and at nine I take a cup of pure coffee, and remain in harness until four. I then take a bath, and go out, and after dinner return to bed. Profit is slow, and debts are inexorable, but I am certain now of immense wealth. I have but to wait and work for three years."

In the following year, he wrote,—

"The fiascos of the 'Médecin de Campagne' and 'Louis Lambert' have affected me deeply, but I am resolved that nothing shall discourage me. After the 1st of August I think that I shall be free."

And later on, in the same year,—

"If I but live, I shall have a beautiful position, and we will all be happy. Let us laugh then still, my sweet sister; the house of Balzac will triumph yet."

To his mother he wrote,—

"The day when we shall all be happy rapidly approaches. I begin to gather the fruit of the sacrifices which I made for the sake of future prosperity. In a few months I will bring to you the ease and comfort which you need.... Oh, my dear mother, you will yet live to see my beautiful future; for, in the end, everything must bend beneath the work of him who loves you, and is your devoted son."

In 1835 he wrote to Werdet, his publisher,—

"Some day,—and that day rapidly advances,—we shall both have made our fortune; and the sight of our carriages meeting in the Bois will make our enemies swoon with envy."

To his mother, in the same year, he wrote,—

"Do not be vexed at my silence. I not only have a great deal to do, but I work twenty-one hours and a half daily. A letter is not only a loss of money, but an hour's sleep and a drop of blood."

To Madame Hanska he wrote,—

"That you may know the extent of my courage, I must tell you that the 'Secret des Ruggieri' was written in one night, 'La Vieille Fille' in three, and 'La Perle Brisée,' which terminates 'L'Enfant Maudit,' was composed in a few hours of mental and physical agony. It is my Brienne, my Champaubert, my Montmirail. It is my campaign in France."

And to Madame Carraud,—

"I sleep but five hours, and work eighteen. I shall purchase the Grenadière,[21] and pay my debts. I need at least a year to be completely free from debt, but the happiness of owing nothing, which I thought impossible, is no longer a chimera."

In October, 1836, he wrote to Madame Hanska,—

"You do not know the depths of my grief, nor the sombre courage which accompanies the second great defeat which I have experienced.[22] The first occurred when I was barely twenty-nine; and then I had an angel at my side.[23] To-day I am too old to inspire a sentiment of inoffensive protection.... I am overcome, but not conquered. My courage yet remains.... During the past month, I have worked from midnight until six in the evening; and while I have observed the strictest diet, that my brain might not be troubled by the fatigue of digestion, nevertheless, I not only suffer from indescribable weaknesses, but I also experience nervous attacks of the most singular character. I sometimes lose the sense of verticality, and even in bed it seems as though my head fell to the right or to the left; and when I attempt to get up I am as though weighed down by an enormous burden, which seems to be in my brain. I understand now how Pascal's absolute continence and excessive brain work caused him continually to see an abyss about him, and obliged him to sit between two chairs.... But if I do not succumb in the mean time, two years of work will suffice for the payment of everything."

To the same lady, two years later, he wrote,—

"I am thirty-nine years old, and I owe two hundred thousand francs. Belgium has stolen a million from me."[24]

In 1838 he wrote to Madame Carraud,—

<hr>

[21] A villa on the Loire.

[22] The disastrous result of his lawsuit with the *Revue des Deux Mondes.*

[23] Madame de Berny, a devoted friend.

[24] An allusion to the pirated editions of his works.

"I have greater faith than ever in my work. I have been offered twenty thousand francs for a play. Hereafter, I shall devote my time to the theatre; books no longer pay.... You have no idea how happy I shall be in a few years. My gains will be enormous."

A few months later he wrote, —

"My debts and money troubles are the same as ever, but my courage has redoubled with the decrease of my desires.... I hope to remain here[25] for three or four months, and then, if my plays succeed, it may be that over and above my debts I shall have gained sufficient capital to supply my daily bread, my flowers, and my fruits. The rest, perhaps, will come with time."

Continually overthrown, but never conquered, in his letters during the next eight years he seems to breathe the delicious idea of De Custine, that hope is the imagination of those who are unhappy. In May, 1846, however, he wrote to his sister, —

"A series of terrible and unbelievable disasters have happened to me. I am entirely without money, and am being sued by those who were friendly to me.... I shall have to work eighteen hours a day."

These terrible and unbelievable disasters were the result of a debt of ten thousand francs, which he owed to William Duckett, the editor of the "Dictionnaire de la Conversation," who, being in difficulties himself, was obliged not only to sue Balzac, but to obtain an order for his arrest. Balzac, however, was not to be found. No trace of him was to be had at Passy, nor at any of his several habitations, which, though secret to the world at large, were necessarily known to the police. One day, however, a woman, whose advances to Balzac had not been met with that degree of cordiality which she had doubtless expected, called upon Duckett, and told him that Balzac was to be found at the residence of Madame Visconti, on the Champs-Élysées.

In an hour the house was surrounded, and Balzac, interrupted in the middle of a chapter, was informed that a cab awaited him at the door. Madame Visconti, with a hospitality which was simply royal, asked the amount of the debt, and paid the ten thousand francs on the spot. A few days later Balzac wrote to Madame Hanska, —

"You can form no idea of the life of a hunted hare which I have led. Two years of calm and tranquillity are absolutely necessary to soothe my spirit, worn by sixteen years of successive catastrophes. I am tired, very tired, of this incessant struggle. My last debts are more irksome than all the others which I have paid."

But now in regard to these debts, to the payment of which he seems to have devoted his life, it is only natural to ask in what they consisted and whence they came: for they became as famous as Balzac himself; they followed him about like a glittering retinue, and found their way not only into his correspondence, but into his romances, and supplied him with a subject of conversation of which he never tired.

------

[25] At Les Jardies.

Balzac, as has been seen, wished to be considered as much of a Monte Cristo as Dumas himself, and could not, without causing his pen to blush, permit it to be believed that he did not extract from his books the same magnificent harvest which was annually reaped by his rival. The debt of 120,000 francs which had crippled his early manhood was, with his habitual probity, soon wiped out; but the remembrance of it remained, and this remembrance, joined to the annoyance caused by a few creditors, suggested an innocent deceit which would explain why he did not live in a palace and enjoy the splendors of a literary monarch. He imagined, therefore, and caused it to be understood that he was not only immensely in debt, but that the sums which he owed were fabulous; and he talked of them, wrote of them, and increased them to such an extent that it was not long before they became even more celebrated than the prodigalities of his confrère.

His debts, however, both real and imaginary, were finally paid, and their liquidation was the climax of the solitary romance of his life.

About the year 1835, he became acquainted with the Countess Hanska, a Polish lady, of great beauty and immense wealth, whose husband was an invalid. It has been stated—on what authority it has been difficult to discover—that when she accidentally met the author of the "Comédie Humaine" her emotion was so great that she lost consciousness. The better opinion, however, would be that a correspondence, begun on her side after the publication of the "Médecin de Campagne," a work which she greatly admired, was continued for a number of years before they finally met. Balzac paid several visits to her Polish estates, and it is probable that she frequently came to Paris. After her husband's death marriage was naturally thought of, but for the time being there were many obstacles: Balzac's pecuniary position was most unfortunate, while she, as a Russian subject, was not in a position to marry off-hand.

The winter of 1848, as well as the spring of the following year, Balzac passed at Vierzschovnia, with Madame Hanska and her children. He was wretchedly ill, and the physicians had forbidden any kind of mental labor. Incessant work and the abuse of coffee had seriously undermined his constitution and shattered his nerves of steel, but the day to which he had looked with such constant expectation had at last arrived: his debts were not only paid, but the revenues from the sale of his books were magnificent.

For some little time he had been preparing in the Rue Fortunée—now Rue Balzac—a superb residence. His taste in furniture and works of art found ample expression there. For one set of Florentine workmanship the king of Holland himself was in treaty, while his art gallery was the same as is described in "Le Cousin Pons."

While he was in Poland his mother was his general agent, and he wrote to her the most minute directions of everything appertaining to the house, its fixtures and decorations; and finally, on the 17th March, 1850, he wrote from Vierzschovnia as follows:—

"Three days ago I married the only woman whom I have loved, whom I love more than ever, and whom I shall love until death. I believe that this union is the recompense that God has held in reserve for me through so many adversities, years of work, and difficulties suffered and overcome. My youth was unhappy and my spring was flowerless, but I shall have the most brilliant summer and the sweetest of autumns."

Balzac had now fulfilled his two immense desires: he was celebrated, he was beloved. His own income combined with that which remained to his wife—she had, at his instance, made over the greater portion of her fortune to her children—sufficed for the realization of his most extravagant dreams. "I shall live to be eighty," he said. "I will terminate the 'Comédie Humaine' and write dozens of dramas. I will have two children,—not more; two look well on the front seat of a landau." It was all too beautiful; nothing remained but death, and five months after his marriage, on the 20th of August, 1850, after thirty years of ceaseless toil, at the very moment when the world was his, Balzac, as a finishing touch to his own "Études Philosophiques," died suddenly of disease of the heart.

At his grave in Père-Lachaise is a simple monument, bearing for epitaph that "single name which tells all and makes the passer dream;" and here, at the very spot where Rastignac, after the burial of Père Goriot, hurled his supreme defiance at Paris, Victor Hugo delivered the funeral oration.

"Alas!" he said, "this powerful and tireless worker, this philosopher, this thinker and poet, whose existence was filled with more labors than days, passed among us that life of struggles and combats common in all time to all great men. To-day, at last, he is at peace: he has taken leave of contests and hatreds, and enters now both glory and the tomb. Hereafter he will shine above all the clouds about us, high among the stars of our country."

CHAPTER V.

THE THINKER.

"Un écrivain doit se regarder comme un instituteur des hommes." —BONALD.

Balzac, to borrow a Hindu expression, was "an artificer who built like a giant and finished like a jeweler." The groundwork of the "Comédie Humaine" was grandly conceived and admirably executed; and though a few of the balconies of its superb superstructure are incomplete, yet as, happily, masterpieces are ever eternally young, it shows no signs of decay, and there is little danger of its falling in ruins.

For the decoration of this work, Balzac brought a subtle analysis of men, women, and things, and adorned it all with brilliant ideas and profound reflections, of which the saddest were dug from his own sufferings, and not, as a great writer has said, from the hearts of his mistresses.

As everything that he wrote is more or less worthy of attention, a complete collection of his theories and teachings would be as impossible, as an arrangement of Emerson's best thoughts, and in any event would ill befit the unpretentious character of this treatise. For his elaborate monographs on religion, morality, society, politics, science, and art, the reader must turn to the complete edition of his writings; for in these pages the attempt will be made to render only a handful of unsorted aphorisms and reflections, taken at random, of which the majority will be found to touch merely upon every-day topics, and that in the lightest possible vein.

With this brief explanation, for which your indulgence is requested, the crier gives way to the thinker.

A woman is to her husband that which her husband has made her.

It is still a question, both in politics and marriage, whether empires are overthrown and happiness destroyed through over-confidence or through too great severity.

A husband risks nothing in affecting to believe his wife, and in patiently holding his tongue. Of all things, silence worries a woman most.

It is, perhaps, only those who believe in God who do good in secret.

Statesmen, thinkers, men who have commanded armies,—in a word, those who are really great,—are natural and unaffected, and their simplicity places one at once on an equality with them.

Comprehension is equality.

Discussion weakens all things.

Genius is intuition.

The most striking effects of art are but rough counterfeits of nature.

To the despair of man, he can do nothing, either for good or for evil, but that which is imperfect. His every work, be it intellectual or physical, is stamped with the mark of destruction.

Avarice begins where poverty ends.

Dignity is but the screen of pride; from behind it we rage at our ease.

There are certain rich organizations, on whom the extremes of happiness and misery produce a soporific effect.

The most natural sentiments are those which are acknowledged with the greatest repugnance.

The first requisite of revenge is dissimulation. An avowed hatred is powerless.

It is in the nature of women to prove the impossible by the possible, and to destroy facts with presentiments.

Power does not consist in striking hard and often, but in striking with justice.

To stroll about the streets is in itself a science; it is the gastronomy of the eye.

Nowadays, to be hopelessly in love, or to be wearied of life, constitutes social position.

Love is immense, but it is not infinite, while science has limitless depths.

Prosperity brings with it an intoxication, which inferior natures never resist.

It is but the heart that does not age.

The graces of manner and conversation are gifts of nature, or the fruit of an education begun at the cradle.

As soon as a misfortune occurs, some friend or other is always ready to tell us, and to run a dagger into our hearts, while expecting us to admire the handle.

It is frequently at the very moment when men most despair of their future that their fortune begins.

To talk of love is to make love.

A married woman is a slave who needs a throne.

The grandeur of desires is in proportion to the breadth of the imagination.

A husband who leaves nothing to be desired is lost.

There is no greater incentive to life than the conviction that our death would bring happiness to others.

Where there is no self-respect solitude is hateful.

A lover has all the virtues and all the defects that a husband has not.

The more one judges the less one loves.

Chance is the great romancer; to be prolific one has but to study it.

Grief as well as pleasure has its initiation.

Apart from the comedian, the prince, and the cardinal, there is a man at once prince and comedian,—a man robed in magnificent vestments. I speak of the poet, who appears to do nothing, yet who reigns above humanity when he has known how to depict it.

Woman's virtue is perhaps a question of temperament.

To live by the pen is a labor which galley-slaves would refuse; they would prefer death. To live by the pen consists in creating,—creating to-day, to-morrow, forever, ... or to appear to, and the appearance costs as much as the reality.

I have never seen a badly dressed woman who was agreeable and good-humored.

A woman's instinct is equivalent to the perspicacity of the wise.

In France, a witticism is to be heard on the scaffold as well as at the barricades, and some Frenchman or other will, I am sure, joke at the general sessions of the last judgment.

All soldiers look alike.

In love, chance is the providence of women.

Literature and politics are to women to-day that which religion was to them formerly,—the last asylum of their pretensions.

True sentiments are magnetic.

Misfortune creates in certain natures a vast desert, which reëchoes with the voice of God.

It is from the shock of characters, and not from conflict of ideas, that antipathies are born.

When intelligent men begin to explain their dispositions or give the key to their hearts they are most assuredly drunk.

There are but few moral wounds which solitude cannot cure.

When a woman is no longer jealous of her husband the end is come; she no longer loves him. Conjugal affection expires in her last quarrel.

A woman who is guided by her head, and not by her heart, is a terrible companion: she has all the defects of a passionate woman, with none of her good qualities; she is without mercy, without love, without virtue, without sex.

The revelation of chastity in man is inexpressibly radiant.

Misery is a tonic to some; to others it is a dissolvent.

A woman who has a lover becomes very indulgent.

Power is clement, it is open to conviction, it is just and undisturbed; but the anger engendered by weakness is pitiless.

Monomanias are not contagious; but where the insanity lurks in constant discussions and in the manner in which things in general are regarded, then it may become so.

One of the misfortunes to which great minds are subjected is that they are forced to understand all things,—vices as well as virtues.

Beauty is like nobility: it cannot be acquired.

Nothing good is to be expected of those who acknowledge their faults, repent, and then sin again. The truly great acknowledge their faults to no one, but they punish themselves accordingly.

Do not fear to make enemies,—unfortunate is he who has none; but try to give no cause for ridicule, and avoid the appearance of evil.

There is as much mud in the upper ranks of society as in the lower, but in the former it is gilded.

The most superb vengeance is the disdain of one at hand.

Laws are not always so cruel as are the usages of the world.

Historians are privileged liars, who lend their pen to popular beliefs in the same manner that our newspapers express but the sentiments of their readers.

A lover is a herald who proclaims a woman's merit, beauty, or wit. What does a husband proclaim?

A woman's real physiognomy does not begin until she is thirty. Up to that age, the painter finds in her face but pink and white, and a repetition of the uniform and depthless smiles of love and youth.

Science consists in imitating nature.

Through a peculiar mental contraction, women see only the defects in a man of talent, and in a fool but his good qualities.

Love may be heard in the voice before it is seen in the eyes.

The heart of a woman of twenty-five is as little like that of a girl of eighteen as the heart of a woman of forty is like that of a woman of thirty: each age creates a new woman.

Love has its escutcheon.

Man clings to life in proportion to its infamy: it is then a protestation, a vengeance of every moment.

Glory is the deification of egotism.

He who foresees a bright future marches through the miseries of existence like an innocent man led to the scaffold. He knows not shame.

The slow execution of works of genius demands either a ready fortune or a cynical indifference to poverty.

No man can flatter himself that he knows a woman and makes her happy until he sees her continually at his feet.

The Orientals sequestrate their women. A woman who loves should sequestrate herself.

A cornice is the sweetest, the most submissive, the most indulgent confidant that a woman can find when she does not dare to look her interlocutor in the face. The cornice of a boudoir is an institution. It is a confessional minus the priest.

True love appears in but one of two ways: either at first sight, which is doubtless an effect of second sight; or else in the gradual fusion of two natures, which is the realization of Plato's androgyne.

A mother's heart is an abyss in whose depths forgiveness is always to be found.

The practice of religion sometimes causes a mental ophthalmia.

Life is made up of varied accidents, of alternating griefs and joys. Dante's Paradise, that changeless blue and sublime expression of the ideal, is to be found but in the soul; and to demand it from the actualities of existence is a luxury against which nature hourly protests.

It is despair, not hope, which gives the real measure of our ambitions. We give ourselves up in secret to the beautiful poems of hope, but grief stands before us, unveiled.

The most ordinary and respectable of men will, when with others, try to appear the rake.

Human justice is, I think, the development of the thought which floats through space.

Through an inexplicable phenomenon, there are many who have hope, but are lacking in faith. Hope is the flower of desire; faith is the fruit of certainty.

A petty work engenders pride, while modesty is born of great achievements.

The problem of eternal beatitude is one whose solution is known but to God. Here below, poets bore their readers to death with their pictures of Paradise.

It costs more to satisfy a vice than to feed a family.

A husband should never permit himself to say anything against his wife in the presence of a third person.

Love prefers contrasts to similitudes.

The sentiment of wrong doing is in proportion to the purity of the conscience, and an act which to one is barely a fault will assume to another the dimensions of a crime.

Woman lives by sentiment, where man lives by action.

Probity, like virtue, should be divided into two classes: to wit, negative and positive. The former would refer to those who are honest so long as no occasion to enrich themselves is offered; while the latter would refer to those who face temptation and resist it.

Woman, as a rule, feels, enjoys, and judges successively; hence, three distinct periods, of which the last coincides with the melancholy approach of old age.

A lover is never in the wrong.

Distrust a woman who speaks of her virtue.

In love, there is nothing so persuasive as courageous stupidity.

Weak natures are reassured as easily as they are alarmed.

The most incurable wounds are those which are made by the tongue or the eye, by mockery or by disdain.

To two lovers the rest of the world is but landscape.

Expiation is not obliteration.

A virtuous woman has a fibre more or a fibre less than other women. She is stupid or sublime.

Language in the magnificence of its phases has nothing as varied and as eloquent as the correspondence of the eyes and the harmony of smiles.

The slave has his vanities; he would prefer to obey only the greatest of despots.

Customs are the hypocrisies of nations.

It is not enough for a man to be honest; he must appear so.

If a man is superstitious he is never thoroughly miserable. A superstition is a hope.

Expressionless beauty is an imposture.

A lack of taste in dress is a defect inseparable from a false conception of religion.

It is more difficult to explain the difference which exists between those who are swell and those who are not than it is for those who are not to efface the difference.

If a man is clever he will appear at once to yield to a woman's whim, and then, while suggesting a reason or two for its non-execution, he will leave to her the right of changing her mind as often as she chooses.

A woman who is happy does not go into society.

Love is not simply a sentiment; it is an art.

Doubt has two faces, of which one turns to the light, and the other to darkness.

A husband should never fall asleep first nor wake up last.

That expression of peace and serenity, which sculptors give to the faces which are intended to represent Justice and Innocence is a young girl's greatest charm; if it is assumed, girlhood is dead within her.

In the lower classes women are not only superior to men, but, as a rule, govern them completely.

To forestall the desires of a lover is a fault in women which few men forgive. The majority of them see but degradation in this celestial flattery.

When a love-letter is so well written that it would afford pleasure to any third person who might read it, it emanates most assuredly from the brain, and not from the heart.

It takes an old woman to read an old woman's face.

It is easier to be a lover than a husband, for the same reason that it is more difficult to be witty every day than now and then.

The woman who has laughed at her husband can love him no longer. A man should be to the woman who loves him a being full of force and greatness, and continually imposing. Households cannot last without despotism. Nations, reflect upon it!

A man seldom passes without remorse from the position of confidant to that of rival.

When two women could kill each other, and each sees a poisoned dagger in the other's hand, they present a picture of harmony which is touching and untroubled until one of them accidentally drops her weapon.

Study is so motherly and good that it is almost a sin to ask of it other rewards than the pure and sweet delights with which it nourishes its children.

We must handle many lamps of Aladdin before we find that the real one is chance, or labor, or genius.

In the life of every woman there is a moment when she understands her destiny, and in which her organization, hitherto dumb, speaks authoritatively. It is not always a man who wakes this sixth and sleeping sense; it may be an unexpected spectacle, a landscape, something she has just read, a religious ceremony, a concert of natural flowers, the caressing notes of a strain of music; in a word, some unexpected movement of the soul or body.

However malicious a man may be, he can never say anything worse of women than they think of themselves.

One may be both a great man and a wicked one, as one may be a fool and a perfect lover.

The ancients were right in their worship of beauty. Has not some traveler or other told us that wild horses choose the most beautiful among them for leader? Beauty is the spirit of all things. It is the seal which Nature has placed on her most perfect creations. It is the truest of symbols, and the one the most rarely encountered. Who has ever thought of a deformed angel?

We allow others to elevate themselves above us, but we never forgive those who refuse to descend to our level.

The customs of every class of society are more or less alike, and differ only in degrees. High life has a slang of its own, but its slang is termed "style."

A fact worthy of notice is the extent to which we make engagements with ourselves, and the manner in which we create our own lot in life. Chance has assuredly not so much to do with it as we think.

The weakest of thinking creatures is wounded in that which is most dear when performing, at the command of another, that which would have been done unordered; and the most odious of all tyrannies is that which continually divests of intention the merit of its actions and thoughts. The word which is the easiest to pronounce and the sentiment which is the sweetest to express dies within us when we feel that it is commanded. We abdicate without having reigned.

The art of marriage, as of literature, consists solely in graceful transitions.

Events are never absolute. Their results depend entirely on the individual. Misfortune is a stepping-stone to genius, a treasure to the adroit, but to the weak an abyss.

To forget is the great secret of strong and creative lives, — to forget utterly, after the manner of Nature, who knows no past, and who each hour recommences the mysteries of her indefatigable parturitions. It is the weak who live with grief, and who, instead of changing it into apothegms of existence, toy and saturate themselves therewith, and retrograde each day to consummated misfortunes.

There are incommensurable differences between the man who mingles with others and him who dwells with nature. Once captured, Toussaint Louverture died without uttering a word, while Napoleon, on his rock, chattered like a magpie; he wished to explain himself.

Man has a horror of solitude, and of all solitudes the purely moral is the most terrible. The early anchorites lived with God. They dwelt in the spiritual world, which is the most populous of all. Misers inhabit a world of fantasy and delight; for the miser has everything, even to his sex, in his brain. Man's first thought, then, be he leper or galley-slave, is to find an accomplice to his destiny. To the satisfaction of this aim, which is life itself, he employs all his strength and all his power. Without this sovereign desire, could Satan have found companions?

Solitude is inhabitable only by the man of genius, who peoples it with ideas, or by the contemplator of the universe, who sees it illuminated by the light of heaven and animated by the voice of God. To others solitude is to torture as the mind is to the body. It is suffering multiplied by the infinite.

The moral of all things has puddles, from which the world's dishonored, as they drown, throw mud on others.

The study of the mysteries of thought, the discovery of the organs of the soul, the geometry of the forces, the phenomena of its power, the appreciation of the faculty which we seem to possess of moving independently of the body, — in a word, the laws of its dynamics, and those of its physical influence will constitute the coming centuries' glorious share in science.

We are obliged to accept the ideas of the poet, the picture of the painter, the statue of the sculptor; but we all of us interpret music according to our grief or our happiness, our hopes or our despair. Where other arts circle our thoughts, and fix them on a determined object, music sends them flitting over the expanses of nature which it has the power to depict.

Thought is the key to every treasure. It brings to us a miser's joy without his cares.

There is not a forest without its significance, not a high-way nor a by-way which does not present analogies with the labyrinth of human thought. What man, whose mind is cultivated or whose heart has suffered, ever walked in a forest that the forest did not speak to him? Insensibly there arises a voice, either consoling or terrible, and often consoling and terrible. If the cause of the grave and mysterious sensation which then seizes him be sought, it will be found, I think, in the sublime spectacle of creatures obeying the destinies to which they are immutably subject-ed. Sooner or later an overwhelming sentiment of the permanence of nature fills the heart, and the thought turns irresistibly to God.

The more illegal the gain, the greater its attraction. Such is the heart of man.

An out-and-out criminal rarely exists, for there are few among us who do not permit themselves one or two good actions, at least. Be it from curiosity, from pride, for the sake of contrast, or by accident, every man has had his moment of kindliness and benevolence.

When we condemn a fellow creature in refusing to him forever our esteem, we have but ourselves to rely on; and even so, have we the right to make our hearts a tribunal, and summon our neighbor there? Where would the law be, in what would the measure of judgment consist? That which is our weakness is perhaps his strength. To so many different beings so many different circumstances for each act, for no two occurrences are ever the same. Society alone has the right to repress its members. As to punishment, I contest it; the curb is sufficient, and cruel enough at that.

The genius is he who perpetually impresses his deeds with his thought.

When a man feels that he is destined to great things, it is difficult for him to conceal it. The bushel has always crevices through which the light must pass.

Women of the world have a marvelous talent for diminishing their faults. They can efface anything with a smile, a question, or a feigned surprise. They re-member nothing, and explain everything; they become astonished, ask questions, criticise, amplify, quarrel, and wind up by chasing their faults away, as easily as they would a spot with a bit of soap. You know them to be black, and in a moment they have become white and innocent. As for you, consider yourself lucky if, in the mean time, they have not found you guilty of some unpardonable sin.

The fortune of a new word is made when it answers to a class of men or things which otherwise could not be described without periphrasis.

One of the most important rules in the science of manners is that you pre-serve an almost absolute silence concerning yourself. Play the comedy, some day, of speaking of your own interests to ordinary acquaintances, and you will see feigned attention swiftly followed by indifference, and then by weariness, until every one has found a pretext for leaving you. But if you wish to group about you the sympathies of all, and to be considered a charming and agreeable fellow, talk to them of themselves, seek some way of bringing each into action in turn; then they will smile at you, think well of you, and praise you when you are gone.

There is no ease in the gestures of a soulless woman.

Instincts are implacable. If we disobey them we are punished. There is one in particular which the animal obeys unhesitatingly: it is the one which commands us to avoid the person who has once injured us, whether the injury was intentional or accidental. The creature that has harmed us once will be always harmful: whatever his rank may be, however nearly he may be related to us, break with him at once; he is an envoy of our evil genius.

Prudence consists in never threatening; in facilitating an enemy's retreat; in not treading, as the proverb has it, on the serpent's tail; and in avoiding, as one would a murder, an injury to the self-esteem of an inferior. However damaging to one's interest an act may be, in the long run it is overlooked and explained in a thousand different ways; but wounded pride bleeds always, and never forgives.

When two people are constantly together, hatred and love grow apace; every moment brings a new reason for stronger affection or increased detestation.

Love and hate are sentiments which feed on themselves, but of the two hate is the stronger. Love is limited; its strength comes of life and prodigality. But hate is like death; it is in one sense an active abstraction; it subsists above men and things.

To invent is lingering death; to copy is to live.

If men were frank, they would acknowledge that misfortune has never taken them entirely unawares, nor without first sending to them some visible or occult warning. Many have not understood the meaning of these mysterious monitions until after the shipwreck.

A singular fascination attaches to celebrity, however acquired, and it would seem that with women, as formerly with families, the glory of a crime effaced the shame. As certain families boast of decapitated ancestors, so does a pretty woman become more attractive through the renown of a terrible betrayal. We are pitiless only to vulgar sentiments and commonplace adventures.

No moralist will deny that the well-bred, yet corrupt, are much more agreeable than the strictly exemplary; for, having sins to ransom, they are very indulgent to the defects of others. Virtue, on the contrary, considers herself sufficiently beautiful to dispense with any effort at being agreeable; and besides, those who are really virtuous have all a few slight suspicions about their position, and, feeling that they have been duped at the great bazaar of life, their speech has that bitter savor which is peculiar to those who affect to be misunderstood.

The woman who is deformed, yet whose husband considers her figure shapely; the woman who limps, yet whose husband would not have her otherwise; the woman who is old, and yet seems young, are the happiest creatures in the feminine world. The glory of a woman is in making her defects beloved. To forget that a woman who limps does not walk as she should is the effect of momentary fascination, but to love her because she does so is the deification of her infirmity.

In the gospel of women, this sentence, I think, should be written: Blessed are the imperfect, for theirs is the kingdom of love. Beauty certainly must be a misfortune to a woman, for its transient charm is the mainspring of the sentiment which it inspires, and the beautiful woman is loved on the same principle that leads a man to marry an heiress. But the woman who is not dowered with the fragile advantages which the children of Adam seek is alone capable of inspiring that mysterious passion which never wanes; to her true love is given, and with it the deathless embrace of the soul. The most celebrated attachments in history were almost all inspired by women in whom the vulgar would have found defects,—Cleopatra, Jeanne de Naples, Diane de Poitiers, Mademoiselle de la Vallière, Madame de Pompadour; in a word, the women whom love has rendered most celebrated were wanting neither in imperfections nor in infirmities, while the majority of women whose beauty has been cited as perfect witnessed an unfortunate termination to their love affairs. The cause of this apparent contradiction is to be found in the fact that the charm of physical beauty is limited, while psychological attractions possess an infinite power; and this, it may be noted, is undoubtedly the moral of the fabulization of the "Thousand and One Nights."

Suicide appears to me to be the climax of a moral disorder, as natural death is the climax of a physical one. Inasmuch, however, as the moral faculties are subjected to the laws of volition, should not their cessation coincide with the manifestations of the intelligence? It is the thought, therefore, and not the pistol, that kills. Besides, the fact that an accident may destroy us at the moment when life is most enjoyable should absolve the voluntary termination of an unhappy existence.... Suicide is the effect of a sentiment which may be termed self-esteem, in contradistinction to that of honor. When a man no longer respects himself and finds himself no longer respected, when the actuality of existence is at variance with his hopes, he kills himself, and thereby offers homage to the world in refusing to remain before it divested of his virtues or of his splendors.... Suicide is of three distinct classes: first, there is the suicide which is but the crisis of a long illness, and undoubtedly belongs to pathology; then, there is the suicide which is caused by despair; and lastly, the suicide from ratiocination. Of these three, the first alone is irrevocable. Sometimes the three classes unite, as in the case of Jean-Jacques Rousseau.... Suicide was permitted by Epicurus. It was the finishing touch to his philosophy. Where there was no enjoyment to the senses it was right and proper for the animated being to seek repose in inanimate nature. Man's only aim consisting in happiness, or in the hope of happiness, death became a benefit to him who suffered, and who suffered hopelessly. He did not recommend suicide, nor did he blame it; he was content to say, "Death is not a subject for laughter, nor is it a subject for tears." More moral and more imbued with the sentiment of duty, Zeno in certain cases forbade suicide to the stoic. Man, he taught, differs from the brute in that he disposes sovereignly of his person; divested of the right of life and death over himself, he becomes the slave of men and events. To man, therefore, freedom in all things should belong: freedom from passions, which should be sacrificed to duties; freedom from fellow creatures in exhibiting the steel or the poison which disarms attack; freedom from destiny in setting a limit beyond which it can have no effect.... Among the atheists of to-day, the coward alone accepts a dishonored life.

CHAPTER VI.
BIBLIOGRAPHY.

"Habent sua fati libelli." —Martial.

The following catalogue is a list of the works which are contained in the "Comédie Humaine," together with those with which it was to have been completed. The titles in italics are those of the latter class.

Thereto will be found appended a complete list, chronologically arranged, of Balzac's novels, as well as of all his treatises, essays, articles, and plays, together with an account of the different positions which they occupied. Some of these works were published anonymously, several were written in collaboration with other writers, many appeared under confusing pseudonyms, while reference to the original editions prove that the majority of the works now comprised in the Édition Définitive[26] bear dates singularly at variance with those of their first publication. The preparation of this catalogue has not been, therefore, an easy task; and while it still leaves much to be desired, the compiler hopes that it may nevertheless be of some value to the Balzac bibliophile.

First part.—Études de Mœurs.

Second part.—Études Philosophiques.

Third part.—Études Analytiques.

FIRST PART.—ÉTUDES DE MŒURS.

Six divisions.

I. Scènes de la Vie Privée.

II. Scènes de la Vie de Province.

III. Scènes de la Vie Parisienne.

IV. Scènes de la Vie Politique.

V. Scènes de la Vie Militaire.

VI. Scènes de la Vie de Campagne.

I. SCÈNES DE LA VIE PRIVÉE. FOUR VOLUMES.

1. *Les Enfants.* 2. *Un Pensionnat de Demoiselles.* 3. *Intérieur de Collége.* 4. La Mai-

[26] *Œuvres Complètes de H. de Balzac.* Calmann Lévy, Paris. THE COMÉDIE HUMAINE.

son du Chat qui Pelote. 5. e Bal de Sceaux. 6. Mémoires de Deux Jeunes Mariées. 7. La Bourse. 8. Modeste Mignon. 9. Un Début dans la Vie. 10. Albert Savarus. 11. La Vendetta. 12. Une Double Famille. 13. La Paix du Ménage. 14. Madame Firmiani. 15. Étude de Femme. 16. La Fausse Maîtresse. 17. Une Fille d'Ève. 18. Le Colonel Chabert. 19. Le Message. 20. La Grenadière. 21. La Femme Abandonnée. 22. Honorine. 23. Béatrix. 24. Gobseck. 25. La Femme de Trente Ans. 26. Le Père Goriot. 27. Pierre Grassou. 28. La Messe de l'Athée. 29. L'Interdiction. 30. Le Contrat de Mariage. 31. *Gendres et Belles-Mères.* 32. Autre Étude de Femme.

II. SCÈNES DE LA VIE DE PROVINCE. FOUR VOLUMES.

33. Le Lys dans la Vallée. 34. Ursule Mirouët. 35. Eugénie Grandet. 36. Les Célibataires: I. Pierrette. 37. Idem: II. Le Curé de Tours. 38. Idem: III. Un Ménage de Garçon en Province. 39. Les Parisiens en Province: I. L'Illustre Gaudissart. 40. Idem: II. *Les Gens Ridés.* 41. Idem: III. La Muse du Département. 42. Idem: IV. *Une Actrice en Voyage.* 43. La Femme Supérieure. 44. Les Rivalités: I. *L'Original.* 45. Idem: II. *Les Héritiers de Boirouge.* 46. Idem: La Vieille Fille. 47. Les Provinciaux à Paris: I. Le Cabinet des Antiques. 48. Idem: II. *Jacques de Metz.* 49. Illusions Perdues: I. Les Deux Poètes. 50. Idem: II. Un Grand Homme de Province à Paris. 51. Idem: III. Ève et David.

III. SCÈNES DE LA VIE PARISIENNE. FOUR VOLUMES.

52. Histoire des Treize: I. Ferragus. 53. Idem: II. La Duchesse de Langeais. 54. Idem: III. La Fille aux Yeux d'Or. 55. Les Employés. 56. Sarrasine. 57. Grandeur et Décadence de César Birotteau. 58. La Maison Nucingen. 59. Facino Cane. 60. Les Secrets de la Princesse de Cadignan. 61. Splendeurs et Misères des Courtisanes: I. Esther Heureuse. 62. Idem: II. À combien l'Amour revient aux Vieillards. 63. Idem: III. Où mènent les Mauvais Chemins. 64. Idem: IV. La Dernière Incarnation de Vautrin. 65. *Les Grands, l'Hôpital, et le Peuple.* 66. Un Prince de la Bohème. 67. Les Comédiens sans le Savoir. 68. Un Homme d'Affaires. 69. Gaudessart. II. 70. Les Petits Bourgeois. 71. *Entre Savants.* 72. *Le Théâtre comme il est.* 73. Les Frères de la Consolation (L'Envers de l'Histoire Contemporaine). — — (unnumbered) Les Parents Pauvres: I. La Cousine Bette. Idem: II. Le Cousin Pons.

IV. SCÈNES DE LA VIE POLITIQUE. THREE VOLUMES.

74. Un Épisode sous la Terreur. 75. *L'Histoire et le Roman.* 76. *Une Ténébreuse Affaire.* 77. *Les Deux Ambitieux.* 78. *L'Attaché de l'Ambassade.* 79. *Comment on fait un Ministère.* 80. Le Député d'Arcis. 81. Z. Marcas.

V. SCÈNES DE LA VIE MILITAIRE. FOUR VOLUMES.

82. *Les Soldats de la République.* 83. *L'Entrée en Campagne.* 84. *Les Vendéens.* 85. Les Chouans. 86. *Les Français en Égypte:* I. *Premier Épisode.* 87. Idem: II. *Le Prophète.* 88. *Idem:* III. *La Pacha.* 89. Une Passion dans le Désert. 90. *L'Armée Roulante.* 91. *La Garde Consulaire.* 92. *Sous Vienne:* I. *Un Combat.* 93. *Idem:* II. *L'Armée Assiégée.* 94. *Idem:* III. *La Plaine de Wagram.* 95. *L'Aubergiste.* 96. *Les Anglais en Espagne.* 97. *Mos-*

cou. 98. *La Bataille de Dresde.* 99. *Les Trainards.* 100. *Les Partisans.* 101. *Une Croisière.* 102. *Les Pontons.* 103. *La Campagne de France.* 104. *Le Dernier Champ de Bataille.* 105. *L'Émir.* 106. *La Pénissière.* 107. *Le Corsaire Algérien.*

VI. SCÈNES DE LA VIE DE CAMPAGNE. TWO VOLUMES.

108. Les Paysans. 109. Le Médecin de Campagne. 110. *Le Juge de Paix.* 111. Le Curé de Village. 112. *Les Environs de Paris.*

SECOND PART. ÉTUDES PHILOSOPHIQUES.

Three volumes.

113. *Le Phédon d'Aujourdhui.* 114. La Peau de Chagrin. 115. Jésus-Christ en Flandre. 116. Melmoth Réconcilié. 117. Massimilla Doni. 118. Le Chef d'Œuvre Inconnu. 119. Gambara. 120. Balthazar Claës, ou la Recherche de l'Absolu. 121. *Le Président Toutot.* 122. *Le Philanthrope.* 123. L'Enfant Maudit. 124. Adieu. 125. Les Marana. 126. Le Réquisitionnaire. 127. El Verdugo. 128. Un Drame au Bord de la Mer. 129. Maître Cornélius. 130. L'Auberge Rouge. 131. Sur Catherine de Médicis: I. Le Martyr Calviniste. 132. Idem: II. La Confession de Ruggieri. 133. Idem: III. Les Deux Rêves. 134. *Le Nouvel Abeilard.* 135. L'Élixir de Longue Vie. 136. *La Vie et les Aventures d'une Idée.* 137. Les Proscrits. 138. Louis Lambert. 139. Séraphita.

THIRD PART. ÉTUDES ANALYTIQUES.

Two volumes.

140. *Anatomie des Corps Enseignants.* 141. *Physiologie du Mariage.* 142. *Pathologie de la Vie Sociale.* 143. *Monographie de la Vertu.* 144. *Dialogue Philosophique et Politique sur la Perfection du XIXe Siècle.* 145. Petites Misères de la Vie Conjugale.

1822.

L'Héritière de Birague, histoire tirée des manuscrits de dom Rago, ex-prieur des Bénédictins, mise à jour par ses deux neveux, A. de Viellerglé et Lord R'hoone. Four volumes in-12. Hubert. 1822.

Jean-Louis, ou la Fille Trouvée, par A. de Viellerglé et Lord R'hoone. Four volumes in-12. Hubert 1822.

Clotilde de Lusignan, ou le Beau Juif: manuscrit trouvé dans les archives de la Province et publié par Lord R'hoone. Four volumes in-12. Hubert. 1822. This romance was republished in 1836 under the title of L'Israélite, and signed Horace de Saint-Aubin.

Le Centenaire, ou les Deux Beringheld, by Horace de Saint-Aubin. Four volumes. Pollet. 1822. This romance was republished in 1837 under the title of Le Sorcier.

Le Vicaire des Ardennes, by Horace de Saint-Aubin. Four volumes. Pollet. 1822.

1823.

La Dernière Fée, by Horace de Saint-Aubin. Two volumes. Barba. 1823. Second edition, considerably enlarged. Delongchamps. 1824.

1824.

Du Droit d'Âinesse. Published in pamphlet form, and signed "par M. D——." Delongchamps, Dentu et Petit. 1824.

Histoire Impartiale des Jésuites. Anonymous. Delongchamps. April, 1824.

Annette et le Criminel, a continuation of Le Vicaire des Ardennes, signed Horace de Saint-Aubin. Four volumes. Buissot. 1824. Republished in 1836 under the title of Argore le Pirate.

1825.

Code des Gens Honnêtes, ou l'Art de ne pas être Dupe des Fripons. Written in collaboration with Horace Raisson. Anonymous. Barba. 1825.

Wann-Chlore. Anonymous. Four volumes. Canel et Delongchamps. 1825. This romance was republished in 1836 under the title of Jane la Pâle, signed Horace de Saint-Aubin.

Molière. Introduction to Les œuvres Complètes de Molière. One volume. Delongchamps. 1825.

1826.

La Fontaine. Introduction to Les œuvres Complètes de La Fontaine. One volume. H. de Balzac and A. Sautelet. 1826.

Petit Dictionnaire des Enseignes de Paris. Published by Balzac in 1826, and signed "Un Batteur de Pavé."

1829.

Le Dernier Chouan. The first edition was published by Urbain Cabanel. Four volumes in-12. The second edition, entitled Les Chouans, was published by Vimont in 1834. In 1846 Les Chouans reappeared in the first edition of the Scènes de la Vie Militaire.

Fragoletta. Criticism. Le Mercure du XIXe Siècle.

Physiologie du Mariage. The first edition was published anonymously. Two volumes in-8. Urbain Cabanel. The second edition, signed, appeared in 1834. Ollivier. In 1846 it entered the first edition of the Études Analytiques.

1830.

Étude de Mœurs par les Gants. La Silhouette, 9 January, 1830.

El Verdugo. Originally appeared in La Mode, 29 January, and entitled Souvenirs Soldatesques. In 1835 it entered the fourth edition of the Études Philosophiques.

Une Vue de Touraine. La Silhouette, 11 February.

Complaintes Satiriques. La Mode, 12 February.

Un Homme Malheureux. La Silhouette, 18 February.

L'Usurier. First chapter of Gobseck. La Mode, 26 February.

Étude de Femme. Originally appeared in La Mode, 12 March, 1830. It reappeared in 1831 in the Romans et Contes Philosophiques, by H. de Balzac. Three volumes. Gosselin. In 1842 it entered the first volume of the fifth edition of the Scènes de la Vie Privée.

Visites. I. Un Pensionnat de Demoiselles. II. L'Atelier d'un Peintre. La Mode, 2 and 6 April. Signed "Comte Alex. de — —."

Voyage pour l'Éternité. La Silhouette, 15 April.

L'Épicier. La Silhouette, 25 April.

Des Artistes. Three articles. La Silhouette, 25 February, 11 March, 22 April.

La Paix du Ménage. Originally published in the first edition of the Scènes de la Vie Privée. Two volumes in-8. Maure et Delaunay-Vallée.

These volumes also contained:—

La Maison du Chat-qui-pelote, then entitled Gloire et Malheur; Le Bal de Sceaux; La Vendetta, and La Femme Vertueuse (Une Double Famille).

Le Bibliophile Jacob. Le Voleur, 5 May.

Le Charlatan. La Silhouette, 6 May.

L'Oisif et le Travailleur. La Mode, 8 May.

Madame Tontendieu. La Silhouette, 8 May.

Mœurs Aquatiques. La Silhouette, 20 May.

Des Mots à la Mode. La Mode, 22 May.

De la Mode en Littérature. La Mode, 29 May.

Nouvelle Théorie du Déjeuner. La Mode, 29 May.

Adieu. Originally appeared in La Mode, 15 May. In 1832, under the title of Le Devoir d'une Femme, it appeared in the first edition of the Scènes de la Vie Privée, but in 1835 it became incorporated in the Études Philosophiques.

Étude de Philosophie Morale. La Silhouette, 17 June.

De la Vie de Château. La Mode, 26 June.

Physiologie de Toilette. La Silhouette, 3 June.

Physiologie Gastronomique. La Silhouette, 15 August.

Gavarni. La Mode, 2 October.

L'Élixir de Longue Vie. Originally published in La Revue de Paris, October, 1830. In 1835 it entered the Études Philosophiques.

Le Ministre. Prospectus of La Caricature.

Croquis. La Caricature, October.

Une Vue du Grand Monde. La Caricature, October.

Ressouvenirs. La Caricature, November.

Les Voisins. La Caricature, November.

Une Consultation. La Caricature, November.

L'Opium. La Caricature November.

La Reconnaissance du Gamin. La Caricature, November.

La Colique. La Caricature, November.

L'Archevêque. La Caricature, November.

This last fantasy contains the germ of La Belle Impéria. It may be noted that none of Balzac's contributions to La Caricature were signed by his own name, his different pseudonyms being Alf. Condreux, Le Cte Alex de B— —, Henry de B— —, and E. Morisseau.

Traité de la Vie Élégante. La Mode, 2, 9, 16, and 23 October. These articles were republished in La Librarie Nouvelle in 1853.

La Comédie du Diable. La Mode, 13 November. In 1831 La Comédie du Diable was republished in the first edition of the Romans et Contes Philosophiques, but it has never formed part of the Comédie Humaine.

Des Salons Littéraires. La Mode, 20 November.

La Tour de la Birette. La Silhouette, 21 November.

Le Garçon de Bureau. La Caricature, 25 November.

Sarrasine. Originally published in La Revue de Paris, November, 1830. In 1831 it formed part of the Romans et Contes Philosophiques, and subsequently entered the Scènes de la Vie Privée.

Des Caricatures. La Caricature, 2 December.

Une Lutte. La Caricature, 9 December.

Les Litanies Romantiques. La Caricature, 9 December.

La Danse des Pierres. A fragment of the legend entitled Jésus-Christ en Flandre. La Caricature, 9 December.

De ce qui n'est pas à la Mode. La Caricature, 10 December.

Le Petit Mercier. La Caricature, 16 December. Portions of this article reappeared in La Fille aux Yeux d'Or.

La Mort de ma Tante. La Caricature, 16 December.

Le Dernier Napoléon. La Caricature, 16 December. This article, rearranged, forms the commencement of La Peau de Chagrin.

Une Garde. La Caricature, 23 December.

Si j'étais Riche. La Caricature, 23 December.

Vengeance d'Artiste. La Caricature, 23 December.

Entre-Filet. La Caricature, 23 December.

Une Inconséquence. La Caricature, 30 December.

Les Horloges Vivantes. La Caricature, 30 December.

Les Étrennes. La Caricature, 30 December.

Une Passion dans le Désert. Originally appeared in the Revue de Paris, 24 December, 1830. In 1837 it was republished in the fourth edition of the Études Philosophiques, but in 1846 it was changed to the Scènes de la Vie Militaire.

Un Épisode sous la Terreur. Published as introduction to the Mémoires de Samson. Two volumes. Maure et Delaunay. Reappeared in 1845 in Le Royal Keep-sake, and in 1846 entered the first edition of the Scènes de la Vie Politique.

Souvenirs d'un Paria. Contained in the foregoing volume.

Lettres sur Paris. Nineteen contributions to Le Voleur, unsigned, dating from 26 September, 1830, to 29 March, 1831.

1831.

Les Deux Dragons. La Silhouette, 2 January.

La Grisette. La Caricature, 6 January.

Paris en 1831. La Caricature, 24 March.

Un Importun. La Caricature, 24 March.

Un Député d'Alors. La Caricature, 24 March.

Le Cornac de Carlsruhe. La Caricature, 31 March.

Le Dimanche. La Caricature, 31 March.

Opinion de mon Épicier. La Caricature, 7 April.

Longchamps. La Caricature, 7 April.

L'Embuscade. La Caricature, 7 April.

Une Semaine. La Caricature, 14 April.

De l'Indifférence en Matière Politique. La Caricature, 14 April.

Le Réquisitionnaire. Originally appeared in the Revue de Paris, 23 February, 1831. It was republished, same year, in the Romans et Contes Philosophiques, and in 1846 was collected in the Études Philosophiques.

L'Enfant Maudit. First part originally appeared in the Revue des Deux Mondes, January, 1831. It was republished the same year in the Romans et Contes, and was subsequently collected in the Études Philosophiques.

Des Signes Particuliers. La Caricature, 21 April.

Les Proscrits. Originally appeared in the Revue de Paris, May, 1831; was republished in the Romans et Contes. In 1835 it formed, with Louis Lambert and Séraphita, a volume entitled Le Livre Mystique. Werdet. In 1840 it entered the

Études Philosophiques.

Enquête sur la Politique des Deux Ministères. Published in pamphlet form, and signed M. de Balzac, électeur éligible. April, 1831. A. Levavaseur.

Tableau d'un Intérieur de Famille. La Caricature, 12 May.

Le Provincial. La Caricature, 12 May.

Inconvénients de la Presse. La Caricature, 12 May.

Le Patriotisme de Clarice. La Caricature, 26 May.

Un Pantalon de Poil de Chèvre. La Caricature, 27 May.

Le Suicide d'un Poëte (a fragment of La Peau de Chagrin). Was published originally in the Revue de Paris, May, 1831. The entire work appeared in August of the same year in two volumes. Gosselin. It was subsequently collected in the Études Philosophiques.

Un Déjeuner sous le Pont Royal. La Caricature, 2 June.

Ordre Public. La Caricature, 9 June.

Une Séance à l'Hôtel Bullion. La Caricature, 16 June.

Conseil des Ministres. La Caricature, 16 June.

Croquis. La Caricature, 16 June.

La Belle Impéria. Revue de Paris, 7 June.

Dom Pedro II. La Caricature, 23 June.

Manière de faire Émeute. La Caricature, 23 June.

Un Conspirateur Moderne. La Caricature, 21 July.

Physiologie des Positions. La Caricature, 21 July.

Rondo Brillant et Facile à l'Usage des Commençants en Politique. La Caricature, 28 July.

Le Banquier. La Caricature, 4 August.

Le Chef d'Œuvre Inconnu. Published originally in L'Artiste, it was subsequently inserted in the Études Philosophiques.

Physiologie de l'Adjoint. La Caricature, 11 August.

Deux Rencontres en un An. La Caricature, 11 August.

Les Grands Acrobates. La Caricature, 18 August.

Un Fait Personnel. La Caricature, 18 August.

L'Auberge Rouge. Appeared originally in the Revue de Paris, 10 and 27 August. It was subsequently inserted in the Études Philosophiques.

Le Claquer. La Caricature, 8 September.

Vingt et Un Septembre, 1822. La Caricature, 22 September.

Jésus-Christ en Flandre. First appeared in the Romans et Contes Philosophiques. In 1845 it was inserted among the Études Philosophiques.

Le Sous-Préfet. La Caricature, 6 October.

Exaltation des Ministres. La Caricature, 6 October.

Moralité d'une Bouteille de Champagne. La Caricature, 20 October.

Études Critiques. La Caricature, 3 November.

Physiologie du Cigare. La Caricature, 10 November.

La Fortune en 1831. La Caricature, 17 November.

Grand Concert Vocal. La Caricature, 24 November.

L'Embarras du Choix. La Caricature, 1 December.

Les Six Degrés du Crime et de la Vertu. La Caricature, 15 December.

Détails Inédits. La Caricature, 29 December.

Maître Cornélius. Originally published in the Revue de Paris, was afterwards inserted among the Études Philosophiques.

1832.

Une Journée du Nez de M. d'Argout. La Caricature, 12 January.

Deux Destinées d'Homme. La Caricature, 26 January.

Religion Saint-Simonienne. La Caricature, 26 January.

Le Départ. A sketch published in a book entitled L'Émeraude. Urbain Canel.

Histoire du Chevalier de Beauvoir, and Le Grand d'Espagne. Originally appeared in an article entitled Conversation entre Onze Heures et Minuit. These two stories were afterwards inserted in La Muse du Département. Conversation entre Onze Heures et Minuit formed part of a volume entitled Les Contes Bruns, which was published anonymously by Balzac, Philarète Chasles, and Charles Rabou.

La Maîtresse de Notre Colonel. An extract from Conversation entre Onze Heures et Minuit. It was afterwards inserted in Autre Étude de Femme.

Départ d'une Diligence. La Caricature, 9 February.

Voilà mon Homme. La Caricature, 23 February.

Madame Firmiani. Originally appeared in the Revue de Paris, February, 1832. In the same year it was published in the Nouveaux Contes Philosophiques de Balzac, and entered in 1842 the fifth edition of the Scènes de la Vie Privée.

Le Message. Originally appeared in the Revue des Deux Mondes, 15 February, 1832. In 1842 it entered the fifth edition of the Scènes de la Vie Privée.

Le Colonel Chabert. Originally entitled La Comtesse à Deux Maris. This story first appeared in L'Artiste, February and March, 1832. It reappeared the same year in Salmigundis, a collection of nouvellesby different authors, published by Fournier Jeune, in twelve volumes, and in 1844 entered the third edition of the Scènes de la Vie Parisienne.

Procès de la Caricature. La Caricature, 15 March.

Sur la Destruction Projetée du Monument du Duc de Berry. Le Rénovateur, 31 March.

Le Philipotin. La Caricature, 22, 29 March and 5 April.

Terme d'Avril. La Caricature, 19 April.

La Vie d'une Femme. Le Rénovateur, 19 May.

Facéties Cholériques. La Caricature, 26 April.

Contes Drolatiques, Premier Dizain. One volume in-8. Charles Gosselin, April, 1832.

Le Refus. Published with other stories, by different authors, in a book entitled Le Saphir. Urbain Canel, 1832.

Le Curé de Tours. First published in the second edition of the Scènes de la Vie Privée. In 1843 it was changed to the Scènes de la Vie de Province, third edition.

La Grande Bretèche. First published in the second edition of the Scènes de la Vie Privée, and entitled Le Conseil. Under this heading was also grouped Le Message.

La Bourse. First published in the second edition of the Scènes de la Vie Privée; it was afterwards inserted in the Scènes de la Vie Parisienne, but in 1845 it was replaced among the Scènes de la Vie Privée, fifth edition.

Sur la Situation du Parti Royaliste. Le Rénovateur, 26 May.

La Femme Abandonnée. First published in the Revue de Paris, September, 1832. In 1833 it was republished among the Scènes de la Vie de Province, first edition, and in 1842 was changed to the Scènes de la Vie Privée.

Lettre à Charles Nodier. Revue de Paris, October.

Louis Lambert. Appeared originally among the Nouveaux Contes Philosophiques. Greatly augmented, it reappeared in 1835 in Le Livre Mystique. In 1846 it entered the fifth edition of the Études Philosophiques.

Voyage à Java. Revue de Paris, November, 1832. Republished in 1855 in the same volume as Les Paysans. It does not, however, form part of the Comédie Humaine.

La Grenadière. Revue de Paris, October, 1832. Republished in the Scènes de la Vie de Province, it was in 1842 collected among the Scènes de la Vie Privée, fifth edition.

Les Marana. Under the title of Histoire de Madame Diard this story was first published in the Revue de Paris, October, 1832. It reappeared among the Scènes de la Vie Parisienne, first edition; but in 1846 it was definitely inserted among the Études Philosophiques.

1833.

Histoire des Treize. Three divisions. The first, Ferragus, appeared with preface in the Revue de Paris, March, 1833. The second, La Duchesse de Langeais, was commenced, but not finished, in the Écho de la France, under the title of Ne Touchez pas à la Hache, and published in its entirety in the first edition of the Scènes de la Vie Parisienne. The third, La Fille aux Yeux d'Or, first announced under the title of La Fille aux Yeux Rouges, originally appeared in the first edition of Scènes de la Vie Parisienne.

Le Prosne du Joyeulx Curé de Meudon. First appeared in La Bagatelle, 13 June. It subsequently reappeared among Les Contes Drolatiques, Deuxième Dizain. One volume. Gosselin, July, 1833.

Théorie de la Démarche. Europe Littéraire, August and September, 1833. In 1855 it was republished in one volume in-18. Eugène Didier.

Persévérance d'Amour. First appeared in Europe Littéraire, 8 September. In 1837 it reappeared among the Contes Drolatiques, Troisième Dizain. One volume in-8. Werdet.

Le Médecin de Campagne. Originally published by Maure et Delaunay. Two volumes in-8 in September, 1833. In 1846 this work appeared in the first edition of Scènes de la Vie de Campagne.

Eugénie Grandet. First published in the first edition of the Scènes de la Vie de Province.

L'Illustre Gaudissart. First published in the first edition of the Scènes de la Vie de Province.

1834.

Séraphita. The publication of this work was begun in the Revue de Paris, but appeared for the first time complete in Le Livre Mystique. Two volumes. Werdet. In 1846 it entered the fifth edition of the Études Philosophiques.

La Recherche de l'Absolu. This work originally appeared among the Scènes de la Vie Privée. It was reprinted by Charpentier under the title of Balthazar Claës. In 1845 it was inserted among the Études Philosophiques.

La Femme de Trente Ans. Six divisions. The first, Premières Fautes, appeared in the Revue des Deux Mondes in September, 1831, under the title of Le Rendez-vous. The second, Souffrances Inconnues, appeared in the fourth volume of the third edition of the Scènes de la Vie Privée, 1834, as did also the third, À Trente Ans. The fourth, Le Doigt de Dieu, was published in two parts: the first, bearing the same title, in the Revue de Paris, March, 1831; the second, entitled La Vallée du Torrent, in the fourth volume of the third edition of the Scènes de la Vie Privée, 1834. The fifth division, Les Deux Rencontres, appeared in the Revue de Paris, January, 1831. The sixth and last division was first published under the title of L'Expiation in the fourth volume of the second edition of the Scènes de la Vie Privée, 1832. Reunited finally under the title of La Femme de Trente Ans, these different headings disappeared on their entrance into the fifth edition of the Scènes de la Vie Privée, 1842.

Le Père Goriot. Originally appeared in the Revue de Paris, in December, 1834, and January, 1835. A second edition was published the same year by Werdet and Spachmann. In 1843 it entered the third edition of the Scènes de la Vie Parisienne.

Lettres aux Écrivains Français. Revue de Paris, November, 1834.

Aventures d'une Idée Heureuse. Of this work, which was to form part of the Études Philosophiques, but a short fragment has appeared. This fragment was published in the Causeries du Monde in 1834.

1835.

Un Drame au Bord de la Mer. First published in the fourth edition of the Études Philosophiques.

Melmoth Réconcilié. First published in Le Livre des Conteurs. Lequin Fils, 1835. In the same year it entered the fourth edition of the Études Philosophiques.

Le Contrat de Mariage. This work, originally entitled La Fleur-des-Pois, first appeared in the third edition of the Scènes de la Vie Privée.

Le Lys dans la Vallée. The publication of this romance was begun in the Revue de Paris, November, 1835, but was not continued. It was published in its entirety the following year by Werdet, and in 1844 it entered the third edition of the Scènes de la Vie de Province.

1836.

La Messe de l'Athée. First published in the Chronique de Paris, 3 January. In 1837 it was inserted among the Études Philosophiques, but in 1844 it was changed to the Scènes de la Vie Parisienne.

L'Interdiction. First published in the Chronique de Paris, January and February. It was changed from the Études Philosophiques to the Scènes de la Vie Parisienne, and in 1844 was finally settled in the Scènes de la Vie Privée.

Études Critiques. Five articles published in the Chronique de Paris at different dates during the year 1836.

La France et l'Étranger. Forty-one articles published in the Chronique de Paris during the year 1836.

Le Cabinet des Antiques. First appeared in the Chronique de Paris, 6 March, 1836. In 1844 it entered the third edition of the Scènes de la Vie de Province.

Facino Cane. Under the title of Le Père Canet, this story originally appeared in the Chronique de Paris, 17 March, 1836. In 1844 it was changed from the Études Philosophiques, in which it had been previously placed, and inserted among the Scènes de la Vie Parisienne.

Ecce Homo. Chronique de Paris, 9 June. Subsequently placed among the Études Philosophiques, under the title of Les Martyrs Ignorés, but omitted in the Édition Définitive.

L'Enfant Maudit. Second part. Chronique de Paris, 9 October. In 1846 this work was published complete in the fifth edition of the Études Philosophiques.

La Vieille Fille. La Presse, 23 October, 1836. Under the collective title of Les Rivalités, this tale, together with Le Cabinet des Antiques, reappeared in the third edition of the Scènes de la Vie de Province.

Le Secret des Ruggieri. Chronique de Paris, December, 1836. Subsequently entered the Études Philosophiques.

1837.

Illusions Perdues. Three divisions. The first, Les Deux Poëtes, was originally published in the first edition of the Scènes de la Vie de Province. The second, Un Grand Homme de Province à Paris, was published two years later (1839) by Souverain, in two volumes. The third, Ève et David, was commenced under the title of Les Souffrances d'un Inventeur, in Le Parisien, July, 1843, and completed in L'État, August, same year. United under their collective title, these three divisions were placed among the Scènes de la Vie de Province.

Les Employés. Originally entitled La Femme Supérieure. La Presse, 1-14 July, 1837. Republished in the third edition of the Scènes de la Vie Parisienne.

Gambara. La Gazette Musicale, July, 1837. Subsequently entered the Études Philosophiques.

César Birotteau. Offered by the Figaro, December 27, 1837, as premium to their subscribers. Two volumes in-8. Originally intended for the Études Philosophiques, this work was afterwards placed among the Scènes de la Vie Parisienne.

Six Rois de France, Louis XIII. to Louis XVIII. Dictionnaire de la Conversation.

L'Excommunié. Supposed to have been written by the Marquis de Belloy, but signed Horace de Saint-Aubin. Two volumes in-8. Souverain, 1837.

1838.

Splendeurs et Misères des Courtisanes. Four divisions. The first, Esther Heureuse, originally entitled La Torpille, and subsequently Comment Aiment les Filles, was first published in book form together with La Maison Nucingen. Two volumes in-8. Werdet, 1837. The second, À Combien l'Amour Revient aux Vieillards, was first published in Le Parisien, May, July, 1843. The third, Où Mènent les Mauvais Chemins, appeared in L'Époque, July, 1846, and bore the title of Une Instruction Criminelle. The fourth, La Dernière Incarnation de Vautrin, appeared in La Presse, April, May, 1847. United under their collective title, these four divisions were placed in the Scènes de la Vie Parisienne. The entire work is a sequel to the Illusions Perdues, and a continuation of Le Père Goriot.

La Maison Nucingen. Published together with La Torpille. Werdet, 1838. In 1844 entered the Scènes de la Vie Parisienne.

Traité des Excitants Modernes. Published in 1838 (Charpentier) together with Brillat Savarin's Physiologie du Goût.

Une Fille d'Ève. Le Siècle, December, 1838, and January, 1839. In 1842 entered the Scènes de la Vie Privée.

1839.

Le Curé de Village. Published in La Presse at intervals from September, 1838, to August, 1839. A second edition was published by Souverain in 1841. Greatly altered, it entered in 1846 the first edition of the Scènes de la Vie de Campagne.

Béatrix. The first two divisions of this work appeared in Le Siècle, April, May, 1839, under the title of Béatrix, ou les Amours Forcés. The third part, Un Adultère Rétrospectif, appeared in Le Messager, December, 1844. This work now forms part of the Scènes de la Vie Privée. Its principal personages, to wit, Camille Maupin, la Marquise de Rochefide, Claude Vignon, and Conti, are generally understood to represent George Sand, the Comtesse d'Agoult (mother of Wagner's Widow), Gustave Planché, and Liszt.

Massimilla Doni. La Gazette Musicale, August, 1839. In 1846 it entered the fifth edition of the Études Philosophiques.

Les Secrets de la Princesse de Cadignan, La Presse, August, 1839. It now forms part of the Scènes de la Vie Parisienne.

Mémoire sur le Procès Peytil. La Presse. September, 1839.

Le Notaire, Monographie du Rentier, and L'Épicier. Published together with a series of sketches by different authors, under the collective title Les Français Peints par Eux-Mêmes. Curiner.

1840.

Pierrette. Le Siècle, 14, 27 January. Subsequently placed among the Scènes de la Vie de Province.

Z. Marcas. Revue Parisienne, first number. Republished in 1841 under the title of La Mort d'un Ambitieux. Now contained in the Scènes de la Vie Politique.

Revue Parisienne. Edited by Balzac. First number, 25 July.

Vautrin. Drama in five acts. Represented at the Porte-St.-Martin, 14 March.

Un Prince de la Bohème. Originally entitled Les Fantaisies de Claudine, it appeared in the second number of the Revue Parisienne. It now forms part of the Scènes de la Vie Parisienne.

Dom Gigadas. Supposed to have been written by the Comte Ferdinand de Gramont, but signed Horace de Saint-Aubin. Two volumes in-8. Souverain.

Scènes de la Vie Privée et Publique des Animaux. Two volumes. Hetzel. Contents: —

I. Peines de Cœur d'une Chatte Anglaise.

II. Voyage d'un Lion d'Afrique à Paris.

III. Guide-Ane à l'Usage des Animaux qui veulent parvenir aux Honneurs.

IV. Les Amours de Deux Bêtes.

Pierre Grasson. Originally appeared in a Babel of collection of romances by different authors. Since published in the Scènes de la Vie Parisienne.

La Femme comme il Faut. Now entitled Autre Étude de Femme. First appeared in the fifth edition of the Scènes de la Vie Privée. Portions of this work are taken from other writings of Balzac not comprised in the Comédie Humaine.

1841.

Une Ténébreuse Affaire. Le Commerce, 14 January, 20 February, 1841. Now part of the Scènes Politiques.

Un Ménage de Garçon. Two divisions, of which the first, La Raboulleuse appeared in La Presse, 24 February, 1841, entitled Les Deux Frères; the second, Un Ménage de Garçon, also appeared in La Presse, October, November, 1842. Both divisions were united under the latter title in the Scènes de la Vie de Province.

Notes Remises à MM. les Députés. Pamphlet. Hetzel et Paulin.

Sur Catherine de Médicis. Three divisions:

I. Le Martyr Calviniste. Appeared in the Siècle, March, April, 1841, entitled Les Lecamus.

II. La Confidence des Ruggieri. Chronique de Paris, December, 1836.

III. Les Deux Rêves. La Mode, 8 May, 1830.

United under their collective title, these divisions now form part of the Études Philosophiques.

Ursule Mirouët. Le Messager, August, September, 1841. Now forms part of the Scènes de la Vie de Province.

La Fausse Maîtresse. Le Siècle, December. Now forms part of the Scènes de la Vie Privée.

Physiologie de l'Employé. One volume in-32. Aubert et Lavinge. Portions of this work will be found in Les Employés.

Mémoires de Deux Jeunes Mariées. La Presse, November, 1841, January, 1842. Now part of the Scènes de la Vie Privée.

1842.

Les Ressources de Quinola. Comedy in five acts. Represented at the Odéon, 19 March, 1842.

Albert Savarus. Le Siècle, May, June, 1842. Now part of the Scènes de la Vie Privée.

L'Envers de l'Histoire Contemporaine. Two divisions, of which the first, Madame de la Chanterie, originally entitled Les Méchancetés d'un Saint, appeared in the Musée des Familles, September, 1842, September, 1843, and October, 1844; the second division, L'Initié, appeared in the Spectateur Républicain, in August and September, 1848. United under their collective heading, these divisions now form part of the Scènes de la Vie Politique.

Un Début dans la Vie. La Législature, July, September, 1842. This work was originally entitled Le Danger des Mystifications. It now forms part of the Scènes de la Vie Privée.

La Chine et les Chinois. La Législature, October, 1842.

Avant-Propos de la Comédie Humaine. Dated July, 1842.

1843.

Tony Sans-Soin. Published in the Livre des Petits Enfants. One volume. Hetzel.

Honorine. La Presse, 17-27 March. Now contained in the Scènes de la Vie Privée.

Monographie de la Presse Parisienne. Two volumes in-8. Mareseg.

Paméla Giraud. Drama in five acts. Represented at the Gaité, 26 September,
1843.

La Muse du Département. Originally entitled Dinah Piedefer, this romance
first appeared in Le Messager, March, April, 1843. Several portions of it are extracts from other works of Balzac not comprised in the Comédie Humaine. It now
forms part of the Scènes de la Vie de Province.

1844.

Modeste Mignon. Journal des Débats, April, July, 1844. Now contained in the
Scènes de la Vie Privée.

Gaudissart II. La Presse, 12 October, 1844. Now contained in the Scènes de la
Vie Parisienne.

Les Paysans. The first part, Qui Terre a Guerre a, appeared in La Presse, December, 1844. The second part, in which it is supposed Mme. de Balzac collabo-
rated, was published after Balzac's death in the Revue de Paris, June, 1855. Les
Paysans is now contained in the Scènes de la Vie de Campagne.

Les Comédiens sans le Savoir. Le Courrier Français, April, 1844. Now contained in the Scènes de la Vie Parisienne.

Histoire et Physiologie des Boulevards de Paris. Published in Le Diable à Paris. Two volumes in-8. Hetzel.

Ce Qui Disparaît de Paris. Same publication.

1845.

Une Rue de Paris et son Habitant. Le Siècle, 28 July, 1845.

Un Homme d'Affaires. Le Siècle, 10 September. Now contained in the Scènes
de la Vie Parisienne.

Petites Misères de la Vie Conjugale. A collection of fragments published at
different times. Chlendowski, 1845. Now contained in the Études Analytiques.

Une Prédiction. L'Almanach du Jour de l'An.

1846.

Les Parents Pauvres. Comprising La Cousine Bette and Le Cousin Pons. Appeared in Le Constitutionnel, October, December, 1846, and March, May, 1847. For these works Le Constitutionnel paid 22,074 francs, of which 12,836 was paid for Cousine Bette, and 9,238 for Cousin Pons. Les Parents Pauvres is now contained in the Scènes de la Vie Parisienne.

1847.

Le Député d'Arcis. The first division of this work, and the only one which is by Balzac, originally appeared in L'Union Monarchique, April, May, 1847. The other divisions are by Charles Rabou, and were published in the Constitutionnel after Balzac's death. The Député d'Arcis is now contained in the Scènes de la Vie Politique.

1848.

Profession de Foi Politique. Le Constitutionnel, 19 April.

La Marâtre. Drama in five acts. Represented at the Théâtre Historique, 25 May, 1848.

POSTHUMOUS.

La Filandière. Revue de Paris, October, 1851.

Le Faiseur (Mercadet). Comedy. Represented at the Gymnase, 24 August, 1851.

Les Petits Bourgeois. Le Pays, July, October, 1854. Supposed to have been completed by Charles Rabou. Now contained in the Scènes de la Vie Parisienne.

Lector House believes that a society develops through a two-fold approach of continuous learning and adaptation, which is derived from the study of classic literary works spread across the historic timeline of literature records. Therefore, we aim at reviving, repairing and redeveloping all those inaccessible or damaged but historically as well as culturally important literature across subjects so that the future generations may have an opportunity to study and learn from past works to embark upon a journey of creating a better future.

This book is a result of an effort made by Lector House towards making a contribution to the preservation and repair of original ancient works which might hold historical significance to the approach of continuous learning across subjects.

HAPPY READING & LEARNING!

LECTOR HOUSE LLP
E-MAIL: lectorpublishing@gmail.com

www.ingramcontent.com/pod-product-compliance
Lightning Source LLC
Chambersburg PA
CBHW051446140726
47987CB00006B/2568